PURCHASED FOR THE LIBRARY
BY
THE JENNIE D. HAYNER LIBRARY
ASSOCIATION

Romania

Second Edition

MARK SANBORNE

Facts On File, Inc.

Nations in Transition: Romania, Second Edition

Copyright © 2004, 1996 by Mark Sanborne

Facts On File, Inc.
132 West 31st Street
New York NY 10001

Library of Congress Cataloging-in-Publication Data

Sanborne, Mark
   Romania / Mark Sanborne.—2nd ed.
     p. cm.
   Includes bibliographical references and index.
   ISBN 0-8160-5082-1
    1. Romania. I. Title.
   DR205.S317 2003
   949.8—dc21   2003045757

Text design by Erika K. Arroyo
Cover design by Nora Wertz
Maps by Pat Meschino © Facts On File, Inc.

Printed in the United States of America

MP FOF 10 9 8 7 6 5 4 3 2 1

This book is printed on acid-free paper.

CONTENTS

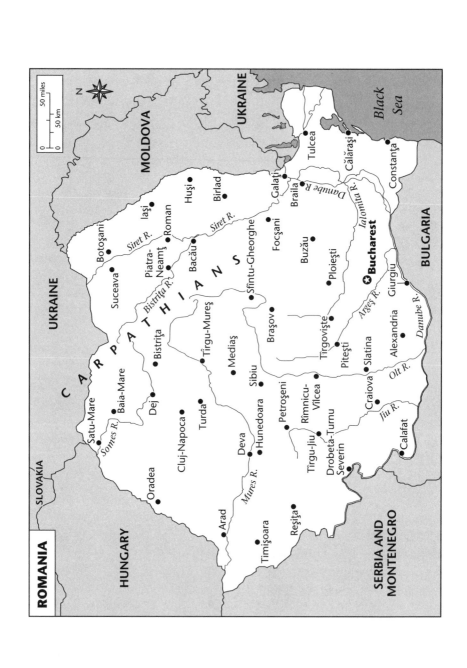

INTRODUCTION

In the seven years since the first edition of this book was written, much has changed in the world. And in Romania? Certainly much has happened, but in many crucial respects not much has truly changed. The question is . . . why?

In November 2002, Romania was given a preliminary invitation to join the North Atlantic Treaty Organization (NATO), the military alliance. That invitation represents the initial step toward economic integration into the European Community (EU). The country still has a long way to go to achieve that aim, but following the NATO summit U.S. president George W. Bush visited Bucharest and officially welcomed Romania back into the fold of "Western" nations. Romanian troops have even been stationed alongside American forces in Afghanistan as part of the United States's "war on terror." Does this mean Romania has escaped its turbulent past and is now ready to join the nations of Europe and the world as a full-fledged member?

That is where the study of history comes in. Understanding where Romania is today depends on understanding where it has come from. In their past, both in a modern state and earlier as the subject of various empires, Romanians have displayed a gift for shrewd diplomacy that has helped their international relations. And yet that same calm sense of intelligence and flexibility has rarely been evident in the management of the country's internal affairs—in matters of politics, economics, and social relations.

The same is true today. Romania continues to make gains in foreign affairs, but until recently in domestic matters the country has stagnated, lagging far behind virtually every other former communist Eastern European country in what matters most to people—their standard of living. Though there are signs that the economy is finally beginning to turn around, serious obstacles remain, and it is unclear how the government will balance its citizens' desire for a decent life with the stringent free-market reforms demanded by the country's international creditors and foreign investors.

And, perhaps predictably, Romania's politics seem trapped in the same time warp as its economic relations. In 1996, angered by their declining social conditions, Romanians voted out President Ion Iliescu, the "reformed communist" who had replaced long-time dictator Nicolae Ceauşescu, in favor of the more centrist Emil Constantinescu. But then in 2000, with the economy in even worse shape, the county voted to bring Iliescu back. Iliescu's return represented, if not a rewinding, at least a pause in Romania's development. All of which raises the question: what is it about this country's past that explains its current predicament?

Romania remains an enigma to most Westerners. During the cold war, Americans tended to think of Eastern Europe as an undifferentiated collection of gray, sullen states suffering under the Soviet yoke. Even with the lifting of the Iron Curtain and the collapse of communism, perceptions have not changed that much. Hungary, Poland, and divided Czechoslovakia are lumped together as modern, if struggling, European states. Bulgaria is thought of as a quiet Slavic backwater. The former Yugoslavia became a synonym for bloody tribal chaos. But Romania does not fit into any neat category, and an air of mystery seems to cling to its history and to its place in the world today. The purpose of this book is to try to explain that enduring mystery.

A traveler to Bucharest in the mid-1990s wrote: "Elsewhere in Eastern Europe people debate how much they're part of the 'real' Europe; but Bucharest seems barely to cling to the edge of the continent, threatening to fall off into some other space, some other idea entirely."

Romania is a nation "favored by nature but persecuted by fate," in the words of a 19th-century Russian general. Blessed with natural resources and a hardy, industrious, and proud people, it is also cursed by its geographic location, which has made it a crossroads of intrigue and invasion by a succession of outside powers. From the legions of ancient Rome to the Red Army of the Soviet Union—between which came barbarian hordes, Ottoman Turks, Hungarians, Austrians, Russians, and Germans—Romania has seen a long line of conquerors come and go. But frequently the country's worst enemy has been its own rulers.

Though tucked away in the southeastern corner of Europe, Romania derives its name from ancient Rome; the Romanian language is a Latin tongue, isolated in a sea of Slavic-speaking peoples. Romanians put great stock in their national mythology—which, though exaggerated, is grounded in history—as a people who can trace their roots directly back to the imperial Roman conquest of ancient Dacia. After bringing civilization, the Romans withdrew and left the Dacians to a thousand-year darkness of barbarian onslaughts.

That was the first of many abandonments that have characterized Romanian history. Romanians are forever being left alone to face some new enemy. They can perhaps be forgiven for thinking of themselves as a "martyred" nation: They were a Christian land dominated for centuries by the Muslim Turks; their Transylvanian heartland was ruled by Hungarians and the Austrian Hapsburg dynasty; they were bullied by an expansionist Russian Empire; they identified with the culture of faraway France but were forced to bow before the power of Germany in two world wars.

Romania has had to perform a delicate diplomatic dance to maintain its national independence since the modern Romanian state emerged in the late 19th century. While impressive in its skillfulness, that dance has often infuriated the country's allies, who accused Romania of opportunism in international affairs. In World War I, Romania began as a secret ally of Germany, switched to neutrality, and finally threw in its lot with the Western Allies. In World War II, after being abandoned by the West, Romania fought on the side of the Nazis before switching back to the Allies at war's end. Then, in what many Romanians viewed as the most treacherous abandonment of all, the Western powers resigned themselves to Romania's domination by the Soviet Union—though some in the West saw that as a fitting punishment for their unreliable behavior.

The wheel continued to turn. When Romania began to pull away from the Soviet orbit in the late 1950s and 1960s, at the height of the cold war, it won back the support of Western nations. As Ceaușescu consolidated his grip on power, the West was willing to overlook his dismal domestic record because he was a thorn in the side of the Soviet enemy. The Romanian people as well were initially seduced by Ceaușescu's appeals to national pride and independence, until they realized that home-grown tyranny could be just as bad as any imposed from outside.

Through the 1970s and 1980s, Ceaușescu and his wife, Elena, ruled Romania like dictators from a surreal farce. They exported the country's wealth to pay off foreign debts while the people scrounged for food and huddled without heat or light. Their "pro-birth" policies resulted in hellish orphanages filled with AIDS babies. They tore down picturesque old districts of Bucharest to build huge, spectacularly ugly monuments to their vanity. They established a cult of personality unrivaled anywhere in Eastern Europe. And their secret police, the dreaded Securitate, cast a web of surveillance over the entire society, to the point where many citizens believed everyone was an informer—and perhaps as many as one in every four of them actually was.

The fact that they had to remain silent in their misery made virtually all Romanians feel a mixture of humiliation and impotent rage. There is an old Romanian proverb of Turkish origin: *Saruta mina pe care nu o poti musca,* or "Kiss the hand you cannot bite." Over the centuries it could be applied to Romania's relations with its various Ottoman, Hungarian, German, and Russian overlords. Above all, however, it is an apt metaphor for Romanians' cowed collaboration with their own misrule at the hands of Ceaușescu. The fact that such continuity is understandable in the light of Romania's history does not make it any less tragic.

The depth of the repression and the pent-up rage, combined with the huge gap between Ceaușescu's rhetoric and the country's dire reality, ensured that the regime's end would be an explosive one. Unlike Eastern Europe's other Communist governments, which fell with barely a whimper, Romania's went out with a definite bang in December 1989. The paradox is that the dramatic "revolution" against Ceaușescu was both the bloodiest and yet in some ways the least politically decisive of the East's upheavals.

More than 1,000 people were killed, including the dictator and his wife. But the faces in the National Salvation Front that took over the reins of power looked suspiciously familiar to many Romanians. That raised questions and conspiracy theories that continue to echo in Romania today. Is the revolution only "half-finished"? Was a genuine popular uprising "hijacked" by a neocommunist cabal of Ceaușescu holdovers led by Iliescu to preserve their powers and prevent real reform and genuine democracy? And why did the center-right and more pro-Western administration of President Constantinescu fail so miserably in solving the country's problems that voters brought back Iliescu—and then only after giving a third of the vote to far-right extremist Corneliu Vadim Tudor?

More generally, what has changed in Romania since 1989 and what has not? At least on the surface, Romania today enjoys more political and social freedom than it ever has before, but as was noted it has been slower to move toward a genuine free market economy than any other East European state. So the short answer is: A lot has changed, and a lot has not. The long answer is to be found in the rest of this book. The first part covers the country's history from ancient times through the end of communism, knowledge of which is vital to any understanding of the Romanian "mystery." The second part deals with Romania's rocky transition to democracy and with life in the country today. The final chapter makes a brief attempt to assess Romania's future prospects.

It is a tale of blood and toil, tyrants and heroes, hope and despair. Most of all, it is the story of a proud and stubbornly persistent people who refuse to exit the stage of history no matter how often the fates seem to conspire against them.

NOTES

p. viii "'Elsewhere in Eastern Europe . . .'" Eva Hoffman, *Exit into History: A Journey Through the New Eastern Europe*, p. 290.

p. viii "'favored by nature but persecuted by fate . . .'" Edward Behr, *Kiss the Hand You Cannot Bite*, p. 34.

PART I
History

1

THE LAY OF THE LAND

It has been said that geography determines history, and this is especially so in the case of Romania. Its location in southeastern Europe, in the northeast corner of the Balkan Peninsula, puts it astride one of the great migration and invasion routes from East to West. It lies halfway between Europe's westernmost point, the Atlantic coast of Portugal, and its easternmost, the Ural Mountains of Russia.

Although it has been both larger and smaller through the centuries because of its tumultuous history, the modern Romanian state has an area of 91,699 square miles (237,500 square kilometers), making it almost the size of the state of Oregon or the United Kingdom. Its greatest distances are about 450 miles (720 km) from east to west and 320 miles (510 km) from north to south. It is bordered in the northwest by Hungary, in the southwest by Serbia (part of the former Yugoslavia), in the south and southeast by Bulgaria and the Black Sea, and in the east and north by the former Soviet republics of Moldova and Ukraine.

The landscape consists of about one-third mountains, one-third uplands (hills and plateaus), and one-third plains. There is an extensive system of rivers, most of which feed into the mighty Danube that forms Romania's southern border. The Danube is the country's economic lifeline, irrigating land for farming and providing a vital commercial transport link to the rest of Europe. As the fabled waterway enters the southwestern corner of Romania, it rushes through a series of narrow gorges known as "gates," the most famous of which is the Iron Gate.

In the northwest of Romania lies the "land beyond the forest"—Transylvania, where most of the country's sizable Hungarian minority lives. Its rolling plains and low hills include important agricultural resources. (Courtesy Free Library of Philadelphia)

Today the river has been partially tamed with a series of locks and dams, but traces still remain of the stone bridge the Romans built during their invasion of Dacia in A.D. 106.

If the Danube is Romania's lifeline, the Carpathian Mountains are its soul. This range forms a great semicircle, running from the north through the center of the country and ending in the southwest. It is divided into the Eastern, or Moldavian, Carpathians and the Southern Carpathians, more commonly known as the Transylvanian Alps. The somewhat lower Bihor Massif is located in the northwest. The country's highest point, Mt. Moldoveanu in the south, is 8,343 feet (2,544 m) above sea level.

The Carpathians are crisscrossed by a series of high river valleys and summit passes that make them easier to traverse than most European mountain ranges. Although well-settled, many of the lower slopes are still covered with dense forests, which are home to wild boar, chamois (a goat-like antelope), bears, and wolves.

Thanks to Hollywood and Gothic literature, this region of Romania is known in the West mostly for its legends of vampires and werewolves. While these mountains are indeed a source of local myth and folklore, their real importance for Romanians has been their historic role as a natural refuge during times of danger and oppression. The mountains were a symbol of national resistance, where peasants could escape the harsh rule of the feudal lords of the lowlands, and where Romanians could retreat in the face of foreign invasion.

The Carpathians also serve a more basic function: regulating the country's weather patterns and climate. The mountain barrier restricts Atlantic air masses to the west-central area of the country, resulting in higher rainfall and milder winters there. At the same time, they block the air masses moving in from the Eurasian plain, so that the southern and eastern portions of the country get less rainfall, colder winters, and hotter summers. Annual precipitation varies from more than 50 inches in the mountains to less than 20 inches in the lowlands. Bucharest, the capital, is situated inland on the southern plain and averages temperatures of about 27°F (–3°C) in January and 73°F (23°C) in July.

To understand Romania's history, one must first become acquainted with the country's three major regions (Moldavia, Walachia, and Transylvania) and three other smaller regions (Banat, Bukovina, and Dobruja). They no longer serve any real governmental function, as the highly centralized modern state is officially divided into 42 separate *judete*, or districts. But these six diverse regions, each with its own district geography and history, remain for Romanians the most meaningful divisions of their country.

Moldavia, located in the northeast, stretches from the Eastern Carpathians to the Prut River, which forms the border with what used to be the Soviet Union. (The Prut is known in Romanian as the *riu blastemat*, the "accursed river," because over the centuries so many invaders from the Eurasian steppes crossed it on their way west, pausing only to slaughter the local peasants and lay waste to the countryside.) Ranging from high peaks in the west to a level plain in the east, Moldavia is the most heavily forested part of Romania.

Farther east, between the Prut and Dniester Rivers, lies the region formerly known as Bessarabia, after a 14th-century Moldavian prince, Bessarab. Long contested for by the Turks, the Russians, and the Romanians, this territory today is the formerly Soviet and now independent republic of Moldova, the majority of whose population are ethnic Romanians. It was briefly united with Greater Romania during the period between World Wars I and II.

Walachia runs south from the Transylvania Alps to the Danube River. It is divided by the Olt River into two regions. The larger eastern section is known as Muntenia; Bucharest is located there. The smaller western section is known as Oltenia. Blessed with rich soil and well-watered by the Danube's floodplain, Walachia contains the country's best farmland.

On the other side of the great curve of the Carpathians lies the "land beyond the forest"—Transylvania. It stretches from the center of the country to the northwest and consists mostly of rolling plains and low hills. Although its soil is poorer than Walachia's, it is still an important agricultural region and also contains large deposits of natural gas and salt. Transylvania is home to a sizable minority of ethnic Hungarians, and con-

The Olt River runs south from the Transylvanian Alps through Wallachia to the Danube. In the background can be seen the famous Cozia Monastery, which was founded by Mircea the Old in 1388. (Courtesy Free Library of Philadelphia)

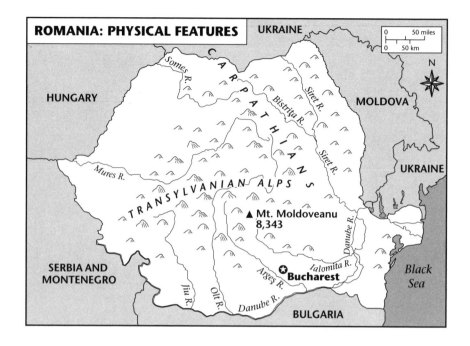

ROMANIA: PHYSICAL FEATURES

UKRAINE

HUNGARY

MOLDOVA

UKRAINE

SERBIA AND
MONTENEGRO

Black
Sea

BULGARIA

▲ Mt. Moldoveanu
8,343

Bucharest

Somes R.
Mures R.
Bistrita R.
Siret R.
Siret R.
Danube R.
Ialomita R.
Arges R.
Jiu R.
Olt R.
Danube R.

CARPATHIANS

TRANSYLVANIAN ALPS

0   50 miles
0   50 km

N

trol of the disputed region has shifted back and forth over the centuries between Hungary and Romania.

Banat, which means "frontier province," is a fertile plain located in the southwest corner of Romania. It is bounded by the Transylvanian Alps in the east, the Danube in the south, the Tisza River in the west, and the Mures River in the north. In the opposite corner of the country, the northeast, is Bukovina, a mountainous, forested region between the Carpathians and Moldavia, to which it was attached politically in ancient times. Romanians, Jews, Ukrainians, Poles, and Germans lived together there in a cosmopolitan culture; one writer described the Bukovina of his youth as "a country inhabited by people and books." It came under the control of Austria for several centuries, and its northern portion was seized by the Soviet Union earlier in this century.

Finally there is Dobruja, a marshy area in Romania's southeast corner along the Black Sea coast. Bulgaria has controlled this region at times in the past. Its northern part consists of the vast Danube River delta, which provides much of the country's fish production. It also contains a wildlife preserve that offers refuge to many rare plant and animal species, particularly waterfowl. Today this unspoiled part of Romania serves as a magnet for migrating birds. But in ancient times, the country as a whole attracted less welcome migrations of a different sort, as we shall see in the next chapter.

Romania's geography has shaped Romanians' views of themselves, as many of the country's intellectuals and artists have noted. "A national history consisting of a series of catastrophes, a geographic position at the crossroads of East and West, directly in the path—and at the mercy—of interests more powerful than one's own: all this probably teaches caution," writer Norman Manea observed. "What can you do? You have to survive."

But if the land has been a cause for misfortune, it is also a source of deep emotion, especially to those who have left it behind when fleeing into exile. The poet Andrei Codrescu wrote, "There is an untranslatable Romanian word that expresses with great precision the kind of unbearable longing and nostalgia that grips one's heart when thinking of home. That word is *dor*. I have felt it many times."

When Codrescu returned to his beloved homeland after the 1989 revolution, he made a pilgrimage to his birthplace in Transylvania. He wrote:

We passed small villages dominated by spires of wooden churches. Now and then we saw roadside shrines, big stone crosses with little huts to pray in. They marked places where travelers died, where battles were fought, where miracles occurred. The country we were driving through had seen thousands of years of wars, conquests, refugees, invasions, migrations. The simple faith embodied in the roadside shrines kept the people going through all of it.

NOTES

p. 7 "'a country inhabited by people and books. . . .'" Norman Manea, *On Clowns: The Dictator and the Artist*, p. 23.

p. 8 "'A national history consisting of a series of catastrophes . . .'" Norman Manea, p. 17.

p. 8 "'There is an untranslatable Romanian word . . .'" Andrei Codrescu, *The Hole in the Flag*, p. 177.

p. 8 "'We passed small villages . . .'" Andrei Codrescu, pp. 150–151.

2

FROM ANCIENT TIMES TO THE EARLY MODERN STATE

To begin at the beginning: There is archaeological evidence of human habitation of the territory of present-day Romania as far back as 100,000 years ago, when Neanderthal people huddled in caves across Europe amid the advancing and retreating glaciers of the Ice Age. In late Neolithic (New Stone Age) times, the local population became intermixed with invading Indo-European nomads from the east, eventually giving rise to the tribes known by the early Greeks as Thracians.

Beginning in the seventh century B.C., Greek colonists founded settlements along the Black Sea coast of Dobruja near the mouth of the Danube, at Tomi (present-day Constanţa) and Callatis (today's Mangalia). The Greeks traded with and influenced the culture of the Getae, a relatively advanced Thracian tribe living north of the Danube. Although a sedentary people, living in villages and raising crops, the Getae were not averse to fighting. Ovid, the famous Roman poet who was exiled to Tomi (he died there in A.D. 16), wrote that the Getae farmers had to wield a sword in one hand while steering their plows with the other in order to defend themselves from raids by fierce Scythian horsemen from the Eurasian plains.

The Roman Conquest

Eventually, the Getae organized themselves into a kingdom, and found themselves in conflict with the growing power of Rome, which had succeeded ancient Greece as the major civilization of the Mediterranean basin. The Romans referred to the Getae lands as Dacia, and coveted them for their gold and silver mines and agricultural plenty.

Two centuries of back-and-forth skirmishes and treaties followed the Dacians' bold invasion of Roman territory in the western Balkans in 112 B.C. Finally, Emperor Trajan decided that Rome had had enough, and in A.D. 101 he launched the first of his campaigns to subdue Dacia, building bridges across the Danube and conquering its southern portions—Banat and Walachia. After the restless Dacians rebelled under their great king, Decebalus, Trajan finished the job in a hard-fought war in A.D. 105–106, capturing the heart of the Dacian kingdom in Transylvania.

The importance of the victory to the Roman Empire was commemorated by the erection of the famed Trajan's Column in Rome, an imposing monument that still stands today, decorated with raised bas-reliefs showing detailed scenes of the conquest. (A similar, though smaller column was raised at Adamclisi in Dobruja.)

The Romans named their newest province Dacia Felix—Happy Dacia—and for the next century and a half it played an important role in their empire, supplying it with grain, gold, silver, and other minerals. The Romans imported colonists from all across the empire, some of whom undoubtedly intermarried with the Dacians. The newcomers built roads and cities, the ruins of which can still be seen today. But the most permanent legacy Rome left was her language.

The Vulgar, or common, Latin of the garrisoned troops and colonists first became the language of administration and commerce and gradually became widely spoken by the entire populace. By the time Rome withdrew from Dacia, its people had a common language. It was one of the few unifying characteristics that would provide the Daco-Romanians with a national identity through the millennium of turmoil and upheaval that was to come.

The importance of this legacy cannot be overemphasized. The name *Romania* obviously derives from Rome, and modern Romanians are fiercely proud of their heritage from classic civilization, believing it sets

The ruins of the fortress of Sarmisegetuza in the Orestie Mountains: This was the stronghold of the ancient Dacian king Decebalus, who fought the Romans in A.D. *105–106.* (Courtesy Romanian National Tourist Office, New York)

them apart from—and above—their benighted neighbors. Although it has absorbed many Slavic words, modern Romanian is a Romance language, like Italian or French, and thanks to the persistence of the mother tongue of the Roman legionnaires, Romania today remains a "Latin island" in a sea of Slavic and Magyar (Hungarian) languages.

Not all the people of the region were "happy" with Rome's domination, and the province continued to be harassed by "free Dacians" from the north and east who allied themselves with other warlike tribes. When the great migrations of barbarian hordes from the Eurasian plains began in the mid-third century, Rome realized its defensive borders were overextended. In A.D. 271, Emperor Aurelian ordered Roman soldiers and colonists to withdraw south of the Danube.

The Dark Ages: Invasions from the East

Some of the colonists probably stayed behind, although there is no firm record of this. In fact, there is little documented history at all of what occurred in Romania in the dark ages that followed, leaving much room for speculation by historians. What is known is that a seemingly unending series of invasions occurred, first by Germanic tribes: Visigoths, Huns, Ostrogoths, Gepids, Lombards, and Avars.

From the third to the sixth centuries, the sequence was the same. Fierce bands of warriors would sweep across the countryside, pausing on their way to richer lands to the west and south, imposing a brutal but temporary occupation. Before they could become firmly established or leave anything of importance behind, another horde would descend from the east, pushing out the previous occupants.

What became of the original Daco-Romanian population during this dismal period is an open question, although it is thought that many of them may have hidden themselves in the Carpathian Mountains, a natural sanctuary from rampaging horsemen. Meanwhile, in the more accessible regions, the Roman towns were abandoned, the roads built by Roman engineers crumbled from disuse, and peasant life in the countryside degenerated into a grim cycle of violence and hunger.

Beginning in the sixth century, and continuing over the next 300 years, the former Dacian lands were flooded with fresh waves of immigration, this time by Slavic tribes. The Slavs, however, came not as conquerors but mostly as land-seeking peasants who settled in villages and intermarried with the Daco-Romanians. Aside from their contributions to the Romanian language, the Slavs also brought another key influence: religion. Farther south, the Slavs founded the Bulgar Empire, which in 676 absorbed much of the southern reaches of ancient Dacia. After the Bulgars converted to Christianity in 864, the Romanians followed suit, adopting the Slavonic-language rite of what later became the Orthodox Church, a rite they maintained until the 17th century, when Romanian became the language of the Orthodox liturgy.

Magyar Rule in Transylvania

The last major invasion from the east that had a lasting effect on Romanian history occurred in 896, when the Magyars—a Mongolian-Finnish tribe—arrived and settled in the Pannonian Plain north of the Carpathians. They founded the kingdom of Hungary. A century later King Stephen I integrated Transylvania, the heartland of ancient Dacia, into his domain.

From that moment on, the history of the region became entangled with issues of ethnicity, religion, and political power that continue to have repercussions today. Hungarian nationalists, seeking to establish their claim to Transylvania, maintained that when the Magyars arrived there the land was essentially empty—that the Dacians of antiquity had fled or been driven out by the barbarian invasions. This appears to be an untenable claim, however. Hungarian chronicles refer to Magyar struggles with the original inhabitants of the area, the "Vlachs"—a Slavic word derived from the Germanic denoting the region's Romanized population, and the linguistic root of "Walachia."

The ethnic differences were compounded in 1054 when the Eastern Orthodox Church of Byzantium, the intact eastern portion of the old Roman Empire, centered in present-day Turkey and Greece, split from the western Roman Catholic Church. The Magyars were converted to Roman Catholicism and remained faithful to it after the schism, while most of the Romanian and Slavic peoples continued to follow the Eastern Orthodox rite.

The Magyars were not numerous enough to consolidate Hungarian control over Transylvania, so King Stephen and his successors invited foreign colonists to help them settle the territory. These consisted mostly of Szeklers, an offshoot of the Magyars, and Germans, who were known as Saxons. Remnants of both of these populations survive in Transylvania today and maintain their distinctive cultures.

The Hungarians also recruited noblemen from the orders of Western knighthood that had fought in the Christian Crusades against Muslim control of the Holy Lands in Palestine. A feudal order was established as the Hungarians granted land, commercial privileges, and political autonomy to the foreign settlers at the expense of the Vlachs, the native Romanian inhabitants. Only Roman Catholics were allowed to be nobles, and while some Romanian noblemen converted to Catholicism to maintain their stature, most Romanians were peasants who remained loyal to the Orthodox faith. They became, in essence, fourth-class citizens in their own land, their status even lower than that of the Catholic serfs of Magyar and Germanic descent.

This process was accelerated after the brief but calamitous Mongol invasion of 1241–42, which saw the horde led by the offspring of Genghis Khan sweep through eastern Europe, defeat all the armies arrayed against it, and lay waste to the countryside, slaughtering much of the population. Transylvania was particularly hard-hit, and after the Mongols withdrew suddenly, the Hungarian king invited more foreigners to settle the devastated region and ordered them to build fortresses. The long-term result was that Transylvania achieved autonomy from the Hungarian kingdom as the local nobles gained greater powers, seized more peasant land and increased feudal obligations.

After a bloody uprising by both Romanian and Magyar peasants in 1437, Transylvania's noblemen formed the Union of Three Nations, which reduced all peasants to serfdom and recognized the nationality and privileges of only three groups: Magyars, Szeklers, and Saxons. Romanians and all others were only "tolerated," and even Orthodox priests were reduced to servitude.

Yet another peasant rebellion erupted in 1514. Numerous but disorganized, the rebels were again ruthlessly suppressed by the forces of the united nobles. The rebel leader was executed in an infamously grisly fashion in the western Transylvanian town of Timişoara: He was seated on a "throne" of red-hot iron and a similarly scorching "crown" was placed on his head. His body was then torn to pieces and put on display in various towns. So many of his followers—both Romanian and Magyar—were killed that for years afterward the Hungarians could not find enough peasants to recruit into their army, thus contributing to their subsequent defeat at the hands of the invading Ottoman Turks.

The subsequent Turkish conquest brought no relief, as the Ottomans allowed the Hungarian nobles to keep their feudal system intact. In Hungary itself, the peasants' freedom of movement was restored a few decades later, but hereditary serfdom continued in Transylvania until the late 18th century, while a similar situation existed in Moldavia and Walachia.

The Rise of Moldavia and Walachia

Ironically, the Magyar and Catholic domination of Transylvania served as the impetus for the founding of the *voivodates* (principalities) of Moldavia and Walachia in the 14th century, laying the foundation of the modern Romanian state. Ambitious Vlach noblemen, kept from power by their Romanian nationality and Orthodox faith, crossed the Carpathians into the forested regions of the east and the Danube basin to the south, where the political vacuum created by the Roman withdrawal had never really been filled. These émigré noblemen filled the gap by setting up their own power bases where they could lord it over the local peasants. They were joined by peasants fleeing the intolerable conditions of serfdom in Transylvania, although they found conditions in these new lands scarcely more comfortable.

Under their new princes, or *voivodes,* Moldavia declared its independence from Hungary in 1360, and Walachia followed suit in 1380. The Magyars tolerated these primitive new states as barriers against incursions from the east and south, and the Vlach nobles were obliged to pay homage to the Hungarian sovereign. But for the most part the princes were left to rule as they saw fit.

Despite the relative peace that reigned during this initial period, life in Moldavia and Walachia was far from enviable. At a time when England had a functioning parliament and Dante was composing his *Divine Comedy* in Italy, the Romanian lands were in an extremely backward state. There were no significant towns. Peasants lived in villages of mud-wattle huts and dressed in the same rustic clothes that had been illustrated on Trajan's Column a thousand years before. There was a complete lack of education, and even religion was poorly organized. Italian merchants from Venice and Genoa founded commercial settlements along the Black Sea coast, but trading was left in the hands of Greeks, Armenians, Jews, Poles, and Germans, while the native Romanians restricted their economic pursuits to simple agriculture.

The Rise of the Ottoman Turks

In the early 14th century, the Ottoman Turks began their rise to power in Anatolia (today's Turkey). Over the next 100 years, they expanded and steadily chipped away at the already reduced power of Byzantium, the former Eastern Roman Empire, until finally only its capital, Constantinople (present-day Istanbul), remained as the sole Christian outpost in a Muslim sea.

The Turks crossed the Bosporus Strait into southeastern Europe in 1352, taking control of the region known as Thrace, which included Greek, Macedonian, and Bulgarian lands. In 1389, the Turks won a historic battle against the Serbs at Kosovo, and four years later they crossed the Danube for the first time and entered Walachia.

According to some accounts, one of Walachia's few capable and strong princes, Mircea the Old (1386–1418), had sent troops to fight alongside the Serbs at Kosovo. Afterward, the Turkish sultan had Mircea seized and held until he promised to pay tribute to the Sublime Porte, which was the name given to the Ottoman government. Unhappy as a vassal, Mircea fled to Transylvania and enlisted the support of Hungary's King Sigismund for a Christian crusade against the "infidel" Turks. The campaign failed, and Sigismund's forces were soundly defeated at Nicopolis, in present-day Bulgaria, in 1396.

Mircea and his mostly peasant soldiers survived the rout and escaped back across the Danube. There followed a brief respite. The Turks returned to the Balkans in 1417 and forced an overmatched Mircea to pay tribute and surrender territory to the Porte. In exchange, Walachia was allowed to remain a principality and keep its Orthodox faith. Mircea, described by one German historian as "the bravest and ablest of the Christian princes," died the following year.

Over the next 25 years in Walachia and Moldavia there was a succession of 11 princes, as both Hungary and Poland schemed to put their own men in power. The Ottoman's capture of Constantinople in 1453 gave the Turks control of the Black Sea, halting Venetian and Genoese trade in the region and increasing the isolation of Walachia and Moldavia. But Hungarian forces led by János Hunyadi then proceeded to rout the Turkish army outside Belgrade (in modern-day Yugoslavia) in 1456. The victory delayed the Ottoman march on Central Europe for decades, although Hunyadi died of plague shortly after the battle.

Before his death, Hunyadi installed Vlad Tepes as prince of Walachia. He became the infamous Vlad the Impaler. Vlad, who ruled from 1456 to 1462, won his nickname by his gruesome habit of impaling his wriggling enemies—particularly Turks—on high pointed stakes, leaving them there to die slowly.

Vlad was also a capable military commander who won a number of victories against the Turks during his relatively brief reign. However,

THE REAL DRACULA?

Although a number of bloodthirsty Romanian tyrants have earned the sobriquet "Dracul" (devil) over the centuries, it is Prince Vlad Tepes—better known as Vlad the Impaler—who seems to have provided the main historical prototype for Bram Stoker's classic 1897 vampire tale, *Dracula*. (In the novel, the Transylvanian count claims to be a Szekler boyar descended from Attila the Hun.) "Every known superstition in the world is gathered in the horseshoe of the Carpathians, as if it were the center of some imaginative whirlpool," Stoker wrote. He apparently mixed the tales of Vlad's grisly tortures with a real-life 17th-century "vampire," Elizabeth Báthory, a Hungarian countess famous for having murdered 600 young girls and bathed in their blood in hope of retaining her youthfulness.

Modern Romanians have an ambivalent attitude toward Vlad Tepes. On the one hand, he is celebrated as a national hero for his blows against the Turks, and it is claimed that his reputation for viciousness is mostly black propaganda concocted by his Hungarian contemporaries to distract attention from their own failure to resist the Turkish onslaught. On the other hand, recognizing the tourist value of the "vampire" mystique, Romanian authorities tout Bran Castle—located southwest of Brasov in Transylvania—as "Dracula's Castle," the historic redoubt of Vlad the Impaler, although in fact he apparently spent a total of only two weeks there while on the run from his many enemies. The castle is currently in danger of collapse due to cracks in its foundation. (See Chapter 8.)

in creating a centralized, powerful army, he suppressed and alienated many of the boyars, or nobles, who ultimately turned against him. The Turks drove Vlad into exile in Hungary and replaced him with his brother, Radu the Handsome, who served as a docile instrument of the Porte. When Vlad tried to stage a comeback in 1476, the Turks gained their revenge by capturing him, decapitating him, and, fittingly, displaying his head on a stake. Walachia ceased opposing Ottoman inroads, and the main theater of resistance shifted to Moldavia.

Stephen the Great and Michael the Brave

The defeat of Vlad Tepes in Walachia set the stage for the rise of a Romanian national hero, Prince Stephen the Great, who ruled Moldavia from 1457 to 1504. His ceaseless efforts to defend his homeland against foreign inroads, although ultimately unsuccessful, have left him with an esteemed place in Romanian history and folklore, similar to that of the celebrated heroine of medieval France, Joan of Arc.

At this point, Moldavia technically owed allegiance to the king of Hungary, while its geographic location placed it within the sphere of influence of the Polish kingdom. In addition, it faced attack from the barbarian Tartars to the east, all the while being confronted by the greatest threat of all: the continuing, centuries-long march into Central Europe by the Ottoman Turks. Stephen owed his success to his skills as a guerrilla warrior who chose his battles carefully and played his stronger enemies against each other.

Stephen's overriding interest was to use Moldavia as an independent base to defend Christianity against the Muslim advance. To that end, he attempted to ease feudal divisions within Moldavia by centralizing the state under his control. He is also remembered as a patron of the arts who sponsored a renaissance of Moldavian religious culture, including the building of a number of strikingly beautiful churches and monasteries— filled with a unique collection of Orthodox frescoes, tapestries, and parchment manuscripts—which survive to this day.

Stephen's reputation as a champion of the common people enabled him to raise a 55,000-man peasant army, which, combined with his astute generalship, gave him a potent weapon to wield against his foes. One chronicler described Stephen thus: "Master of the craft of war, he went wherever he was needed so that seeing him his men would not disperse and for that reason there was seldom a war that he did not win. And when others defeated him, he did not lose hope, for, when vanquished, he would rise above his vanquishers."

In the 1480s, first Hungary then Poland signed peace treaties with the Ottoman sultan (king), and the Turks captured the strategic Black Sea fortress of Chilia, the "key to the door to all Moldavia as well as Hungary and the whole Danubian region." Abandoned by his erstwhile allies, Stephen ceased his anti-Turkish crusade, and on his deathbed allegedly advised his son, Bogdan the One-Eyed, to come to terms with the infidels if they offered an honorable peace. Wasting no time, soon after Stephen's death in 1504 Bogdan signed a treaty of vassalage with the Sublime Porte, although periodic acts of resistance persisted in the decades that followed.

Stephen the Great's successes have inspired generations of Romanians down to the present day. His eventual failure, however, helped feed a belief that has continued to haunt the national consciousness: that Romania's interests have been consistently betrayed over the centuries by the cynical manipulations of outside powers.

Hungary, meanwhile, which had been weakened internally by peasant revolts and feudal tensions, proved an irresistible target to the ascendant

The famous monastery at Voronet in Bukovina. It was built by Stephen the Great in 1488; the painted frescoes were added later. (Courtesy Romanian National Tourist Office, New York)

Turks. They captured Belgrade in 1521, won a pivotal victory over a Hungarian army at Mohács in 1526, and seized Buda (later Budapest) in 1541. As a result of these conquests, Transylvania became an autonomous principality under Ottoman vassalage, while both Walachia and Moldavia lost their few remaining vestiges of independence.

Turks were not permitted to own land or build mosques to spread the Muslim faith in the two principalities, due to their status as vassal states rather than *pashaliks* (provinces of the Ottoman Empire). But the Ottomans, in league with their local rulers, did allow Turkish and Greek merchants and usurers (moneylenders) to systematically exploit the region's wealth, which had the effect of smothering the small Romanian middle class and further impoverishing the peasantry.

This was the situation that existed at the time of the brief reign of Michael the Brave (1593–1601). He began his rise to power in the traditional manner, by paying a huge bribe to the Porte to win appointment as prince of Walachia. But unlike the mostly servile rulers who preceded him, Michael's goal was total independence from the Ottoman Empire.

Shortly after being enthroned, he signaled the start of his revolt by rounding up a group of Turkish moneylenders, locking them in a building, and burning them alive. He then proceeded to lead his army in a successful campaign against Turkish military forces in Walachia. Searching for allies, in 1598 he pledged loyalty to Holy Roman Emperor Rudolf II, the ruler of Austria's Hapsburg Empire. The following year he marched on Transylvania, routing the Hungarians there, and in 1600 he went on to conquer Moldavia. Michael proclaimed himself "Prince of Walachia, Transylvania and Moldavia," and for the first time the lands that would ultimately comprise the modern state of Romania were united under one ruler.

Although Michael's moment of triumph did not last long, the example he set served as an inspiration for Romanian nationalists in the centuries that followed. His tale, however, was not necessarily the purely idealistic and heroic epic related by later Romanian chroniclers. In common with the princes and politics of his era, Michael's success was built as much on treachery and betrayal as it was on bravery and military skill.

In the end, it was Michael's unexpected success that led to his undoing. Alarmed by his growing power, Emperor Rudolf prompted Transylvania's nobles to launch their own revolt against Michael, while at the same time Polish forces, allied with the Turks, intervened in Moldavia. Michael was assassinated in 1601 on the orders of Georgio Basta, the Hapsburg emperor's general. For a prince with such a short-lived career, his legacy was a long-lasting one.

Transylvania under Hapsburg Rule

For 150 years, from 1540 to around 1690, Transylvania enjoyed an era of autonomy as the mostly Hungarian nobles ruled the country with little interference from their nominal Ottoman overlords. Meanwhile, the 16th-century Reformation—the anti-Catholic religious movement that led to the establishment of Protestant churches and sects throughout Europe—found particularly fertile ground in Transylvania.

In 1571 the Transylvanian Diet (parliament) passed a law granting equality and freedom of worship to the country's four "received," or officially recognized, religions: Roman Catholic, Calvinist, Lutheran, and Unitarian (a liberal Protestant sect that rejected many standard Christian doctrines). Although the law was progressive for its time in Europe, it had one glaring inconsistency: It failed to recognize the Orthodox faith of the Romanians, who remained the largest religious subgroup in Transylvania.

In 1683, the Ottoman advance into Europe crashed futilely against the gates of the Austrian capital of Vienna, after a long siege where united Christian forces defeated and drove off a huge Turkish army. As the Turks' power was gradually rolled back in the decades that followed, the Transylvanian Diet in 1688 renounced the Ottoman overlords and accepted the rule of Austria's Hapsburg Empire. Hapsburg control over Transylvania, formalized by the Treaty of Karlowitz (Sremski Karlovci) in 1699, was to last the next two centuries.

Religious issues and conflicts continued to dominate during this period. The most important development, in terms of Romanian history, was the creation of the Uniate Church in 1699. The Uniate Church (not to be confused with the Unitarian faith) retained most of the rituals and liturgy of Orthodox Christianity but accepted key points of Catholic doctrine, including the authority of the pope. Priests of the Jesuit order, dispatched by the Austrian court, devised the Uniate Church as a means of luring Transylvania's Romanians into the Catholic fold and so increasing its numbers, since most Lutherans and Calvinists strenuously resisted reconversion.

In return for becoming Uniates, the Jesuits offered Orthodox clergy exemption from serfdom and increased social status, although the Hapsburgs did not go so far as to make the new church one of the four "received" religions. However, the development of the Uniate Church ultimately had the unintended effect of sparking a renewal of Romanian national consciousness. Young Uniate clerics were sent to Rome for education, where they saw Trajan's Column and became aware of the classical Roman and Dacian roots of their culture. They brought that knowledge home with them, adapting the Latin alphabet to the Romanian language in place of the Slavic Cyrillic script and publishing the first grammars and prayer books in modern Romanian. The southern Transylvanian city of Blaj, seat of the Uniate Church, became the hub of this cultural renaissance.

Emperor Joseph II (1780–90), an "enlightened despot," initiated a program of moderate reform throughout the Hapsburg Empire to improve the lives of the serfs and preempt revolutions from below. He also decreed that German was to be the official language. These steps backfired in Transylvania, where the peasants rose up in an unsuccessful rebellion and Magyars began calling for the union of Transylvania and Hungary and the "Magyarization" of Romanian and other non-Hungarian peoples.

The situation came to a head when liberal and nationalist revolutions erupted across Europe in 1848. Hungary joined the revolt, abolishing serfdom and declaring the unification of Hungary and Transylvania. This touched off a bloody civil war in Transylvania, with Romanians and Saxons, aided by Austrian imperial troops, battling the Magyars. Eventually, with the aid of Russian forces, the revolution was crushed. Austria imposed a harsh military occupation on Transylvania, under which the Romanian population was no better off than before. Although there was a brief period of reform in 1863–65, by 1867 a weakened Hapsburg Empire was forced to enter into a dual monarchy with Hungary. The result was that Transylvania was yet again united with Hungary, and the Romanians there faced another half-century of persecution at the hands of the Magyars.

Phanariot Rule and the Russian Occupations

From the beginning of the 18th century onward, the history of Walachia and Moldavia was at least as tumultuous as that of Transylvania. The era was primarily defined by the growing conflict between the Russian and Ottoman empires, in which the two Romanian principalities became a constant battleground.

Under Czar Peter the Great (1696–1725), the expanding Russian Empire had succeeded Poland as the most influential power in Eastern Europe. Peter proclaimed himself the champion of his fellow Orthodox Christians living under the Turkish yoke, and in 1711 he attempted to liberate Moldavia. The military bid failed, and the Ottomans, alarmed by the support shown by the Romanian princes for the Russian invasion, instituted what became known as the "Phanariot" system.

The Phanariots were Byzantines, aristocratic Greeks from Constantinople's Phanar, or lighthouse, district. No longer trusting the native Romanian nobles to be sufficiently pliant, the Sublime Porte henceforth appointed only Phanariots to be princes of Walachia and Moldavia. In exchange for their absolute loyalty to the sultan, the Phanariots were encouraged to take economic exploitation of their subjects to a new level, wringing as much wealth from the land and people as possible.

The new system resulted in widespread corruption and heightened economic misery. While the princes and boyars lived in relative luxury, the peasants and even most of the townspeople remained mired in primitive living conditions. An English traveler passing through Walachia in 1747 painted an unflattering portrait of its capital city: "Bucharest is a large straggling town of a very peculiar make, the outward parts very mean, consisting of houses, the greater part of which is underground like our cellars, and covered over at the top with straw or bark of trees."

Most of all, it was a period characterized by a succession of wars, invasions, broken treaties, and diplomatic intrigues. Between 1711 and 1856, at least eight wars were waged on Romanian soil involving Russia, Austria, and the Turks. Aside from the vast human and material losses, these conflicts also resulted in various territorial maimings of Walachia and Moldavia.

Russia invaded the principalities in 1739, 1769, 1787, 1806, 1828, 1848, and 1853, occupying them as protectorates for long periods while gaining greater concessions from the weakening Turks and increased authority over internal Romanian affairs. While initially welcoming them as liberators, Romanians eventually came to see the Russians as just another foreign conqueror, and developed a strong distrust of their giant eastern neighbor that only deepened in the 20th century.

Phanariot rule came to an abrupt end in 1821 after an abortive anti-Ottoman rebellion by Greek nationalists led by Alexander Ypsilanti, son of a Phanariot prince and a general in the Russian army. He and his men seized control of Moldavia, while Tudor Vladimirescu, a Romanian whose military skills had allowed him to rise from peasant to boyar rank, led an anti-Phanariot revolt in Walachia. After their initial successes, the two men quarreled, the Greeks murdered Vladimirescu, and the Turks (with Russia's approval) proceeded to crush Ypsilanti's insurgency. The Sublime Porte, now fearing the loyalty of its Greek subjects, returned to its old practice of appointing native Romanians as princes.

The Union of Moldavia and Walachia

Ironically, for all the difficulties caused by Russia's interventions, it was a Russian general who helped lay the groundwork for the eventual unification of Moldavia and Walachia. Count Pavel Kiselev, who administered the two territories during Russia's 1829–34 occupation, was something of a liberal schooled in the ideals of French Enlightenment tradition. During his tenure, he organized the principalities' first modern police force, medical service, and grain reserves. Conditions in the cities gradually improved, although life in the countryside remained mostly miserable. A traveler in Walachia in 1835 reported not seeing "either manor house, bridge, windmills, or inn, or furniture or utensils in the peasant huts."

Most importantly, Kiselev oversaw the promulgation of the Règlement Organique (Organic Regulations, or Constitution), a system of fundamental laws that provided for princes to be chosen by an elected assembly of boyars and clergy. It also reformed the judiciary and set up the first public education system. Although it included some regressive economic provisions—reducing peasant mobility and increasing peasant obligations to the boyars—the main benefit of the Règlement Organique was to provide both Walachia and Moldavia with identical systems of government, even while they remained separate political entities.

The final spur for unification came from the European-wide revolutions of 1848. Inspired by the uprising in Transylvania, radical Romanian nationalists also rose up in Moldavia and Walachia, seeking independence from foreign domination. The conservative Russian and Ottoman empires acted together to snuff out the rebellions, and many of the radicals fled to France as political refugees.

Many of these youthful émigrés had been educated in Paris and were welcomed back as revolutionary heroes. This attitude was epitomized by a famous remark made at the time by a woman of Parisian high society: "So young and already Moldo-Walachian!" Similarly, a historian drew this romantic picture of the typical Romanian émigré:

> The exile was a young man with long hair, flashing eyes, with a large Carbonari hat, high collar with a scarf wound around it up to his ears and who had only to roll up his sleeves to show the wounds Tyranny had inflicted on him. He was loaded with news sheets, brochures and proclamations. Politicians bowed before an outlaw.

The Russians themselves set the stage for Romanian independence in 1853 when, badly misjudging the international climate, they invaded the principalities yet one more time. This action precipitated the Crimean War, which saw Russia defeated in its attempt to seize territory from the declining Ottoman Empire. The Turks were backed by Britain, France, Austria, and other European powers, which wanted to preserve the balance of power in the region.

Austrian and Turkish troops forced Russia to withdraw from Moldavia and Walachia. Under the 1856 Treaty of Paris, a joint European guarantee replaced the Russian protectorate, and it was agreed that no power was to enjoy "exclusive protection" of the principalities, although the Turks continued to exercise nominal sovereignty. In addition, the treaty freed navigation on the Danube and compelled Russia to return a section of southern Bessarabia, including control of the Danube's mouth, to Moldavia.

These events prompted an active movement by Romanian nationalists for the unification of Walachia and Moldavia. The campaign had the backing of the French government of Napoleon III, thanks to the influence of the Romanian émigrés in Paris. The Ottomans, Austria, and Britain were opposed; Russia proposed to allow the Romanians themselves to vote on the issue. A referendum was held in 1857 in which the unionists lost, but the rigging of the election by the Turks (allegedly with British connivance) was so blatant that it prompted an international crisis.

A new vote resulted in a large majority of delegates in favor of unification. The unionists followed up by issuing a call for a constitutional government to be headed by a foreign prince who would rule over both principalities. But the international community still favored caution, and a conference in Paris in 1858 asserted that Moldavia and Walachia should retain separate governments under loose Turkish control. On the other hand, the conference also named the two states the *United Principalities* (while resisting use of the name *Romania*) and said they could share a common currency and legal system.

Finally, the Romanian nationalists came up with a clever solution to overcome the imposed political division: In January 1859 the separate assemblies in Iaşi, Moldavia, and Bucharest, Walachia, elected the same man—Alexandru Ioan Cuza, liberal son of a Moldavian boyar—as the governor of their respective principalities. Caught by surprise and distracted by a military crisis in Italy, Europe's leading powers accepted the de facto unification and allowed Cuza to become prince.

Further discussions led to formal European and Ottoman recognition of the union of Walachia and Moldavia in 1861. Cuza, who had been shuttling between the assemblies and ministries in Bucharest and Iasi for two years, officially established the nation's capital at Bucharest, the country's largest city. On November 11, 1861, he was able to proclaim: "The Union has been accomplished, the Romanian nation has been founded. As your elected representative, I present you today one single Romania." The following month, with what later proved to be considerable foresight, he remarked, "I fear you will not be satisfied with me for long."

It took a grudging Europe some 15 years to adopt the name *Romania* for the new state, and by then Cuza himself was long gone from the scene.

NOTES

p. 16 "'the bravest and ablest of the Christian princes.'" Andrei Otetea, ed., *The History of the Romanian People*, p. 195.

p. 17 "'Every known superstition in the world . . .'" Bram Stoker, *Dracula*, p. 2 (Bantam Classic edition, 1981).

p. 18 "'Master of the craft of war . . .'" Otetea, p. 201.

p. 18 "'key to the door to all Moldavia . . .'" Denise Basdevant, *Against Tide and Tempest*, p. 23.

p. 23 "'Bucharest is a large straggling town . . .'" Julian Hale, *The Land and People of Romania*, p. 37.

p. 24 "'either manor house, bridge, windmills, . . .'" Basdevant, p. 46.

p. 25 "'So young and already Moldo-Walachian!'" Basdevant, p. 51.

p. 25 "'The exile was a young man with long hair, . . .'" Basdevant, p. 51.

p. 26 "'The Union has been accomplished, . . .'" Basdevant, p. 60.

p. 26 "'I fear you will not be satisfied with me for long.'" Edward Behr, *Kiss the Hand You Cannot Bite*, p. 35.

3

FROM THE LATE 19TH CENTURY THROUGH THE WORLD WARS

Shortly after the official unification of Moldavia and Walachia in 1861, Prince Alexandru Cuza (1859–66) began a bold program of domestic reform. His efforts surprised some observers, as he had been elected as a compromise candidate and had not had a particularly distinguished political career up to that point.

In the face of close international attention, he had to carry out a careful balancing act. The Ottoman Empire regularly threatened to reoccupy the principalities, to which menacing the Russians responded by backing a Moldavian separatist movement. The British worried about anything that might give the Russians an excuse to expand their influence. And the Austrians feared that the new state would ignite Romanian nationalist fervor in Transylvania and Bukovina.

Fortunately for Cuza, the actions of Turkey, Russia, and Britain tended to offset each other, while Austria was preoccupied with the crisis of Italian independence. But most important of all was the critical diplomatic and military support given to Romania by the French government of Napoleon III. Appreciating this, Cuza wrote to his foreign envoys: "Do not let France cool toward us at any price, because, in my opinion, she is the only power on whom we can really count."

Cuza had less success in balancing domestic objections to his rule. Radical elements of the Liberal Party faulted him for not repudiating Ottoman influence and for not working harder to reunite Romania with its neighboring countrymen still living under foreign domination. At the other end of the political spectrum, the Conservative Party, controlled largely by the boyar class of rich landlords, was alienated by his efforts to purge Romania of its remaining vestiges of feudalism.

To outflank his political opponents, Cuza in 1864 dissolved the legislative assembly and took his case directly to the people in a national referendum. Winning a vote of confidence from the peasant majority, he passed a new electoral law granting universal suffrage (voting rights), establishing a more modern legislature, and, following the example of Napoleon III, giving himself essentially dictatorial powers to carry out his reform program.

Cuza rewarded the peasants with an agrarian law that formally abolished serfdom, tithes (enforced payments to landlords), and forced labor. The law also allowed peasants to own land, allotting 2 million hectares (5 million acres) to 400,000 peasants. But in part because of opposition by the boyars, the new plots were too expensive for most peasants and too small to be farmed for a profit. As a result, economic conditions for many people in rural areas actually worsened.

Cuza also carried out other, less controversial reforms. These included new criminal and civil codes modeled on the French legal system, an improved road system, the establishment of compulsory, free elementary education, and the founding of universities in Iași and Bucharest.

Eventually, Cuza's missteps antagonized the ordinary people, who joined with the political elite in opposition. Popular anger mounted over the regime's economic mismanagement and corruption, and over Cuza's increasingly dictatorial and "regal" behavior, along with scandals in his personal life. (According to one rumor, he was attempting to arrange for one of his mistress's sons to succeed him on the throne.)

After the government's brutal suppression of a riot in Bucharest, the Liberals and Conservatives joined together in February 1866 to oust the first ruler of modern Romania. Army officers woke Cuza and his mistress in the palace, forced the prince to sign papers of abdication, and escorted him out of the country.

King Carol I

With the departure of Cuza, the government announced a regency pending the election of a foreign prince, as the unionists had long sought. (Rule by a foreign-born monarch would avoid charges of favoritism toward either Moldavia or Walachia.) After shopping around through the royal houses of Europe, Liberal Party leader Ion Bratianu nominated Prince Charles of southern Germany's Hohenzollern-Sigmaringen family, a choice backed by France's Napoleon III and Prussian Premier Otto von Bismarck. The selection of the 27-year-old prince was approved in a Romanian referendum, and he was formally invited to assume the throne.

Charles—*Karl* in German, or *Carol* in Romanian, as he was subsequently known—feared being stopped along the way if he traveled openly via Russia or Austria, which was on the verge of war with Prussia. So he made the journey to Romania disguised as a common salesman, traveling under a false passport by second-class rail and steamboat through Austrian territory, reaching Bucharest in May 1866. He would rule the country until his death in 1914.

Upon arriving in his new home, Carol was apparently shocked by its backward state. At one point he asked where he was and was told he had reached the royal palace. "Looking at the building and thinking he had not heard correctly, [Carol] asked, '*Where* is the Palace?' His informer could only point in embarrassment to the low building that looked out on an undistinguished guardhouse and gypsy camp, with its group of pigs wallowing in the mud."

During his reign, Carol tried to provide the country with a modern administration, despite a succession of Liberal and Conservative governments that rose and fell in elections that were often corrupt. Among his major contributions were building of the country's first railroad system and modernizing its armed forces, with the aid of Prussian advisers. But in a country overwhelmingly sympathetic to France, Carol also found himself enduring opposition and insults due to his own Prussian origins. The atmosphere reached crisis proportions during the Franco-Prussian War of 1870–71 (in which France was soundly defeated), and Carol came close to abdicating.

During the 1877–78 Russo-Turkish War, the Romanian parliament voted to support what it perceived as the lesser of two evils and came out

King Carol I came to Romania as a 27-year-old German prince in 1866. By the time he died in 1914, he had presided over the most peaceful and prosperous period in his adopted nation's history. (Courtesy Library of Congress)

on the side of Russia. It declared Romania to be finally and permanently free of Ottoman sovereignty and allowed Russian forces to pass through Romanian territory to attack the Turks. When Russian troops became trapped south of the Danube at Plevna (in present-day Bulgaria), the Romanian army, personally led by Prince Carol, came to their rescue and helped rout the Turks.

Despite Romania's crucial contribution to their victory, the Russians refused to let Romania participate in the 1878 Congress of Berlin that settled the issues resulting from the war. In the end, Romania was forced to accept Russia's annexation of southern Bessarabia from Moldavia, while in return it gained control over northern Dobruja, which included the Danube delta. Europe agreed to recognize Romania's formal and complete independence, in exchange for two main conditions: one, that it consent to the territorial deal with Russia, and two, that it guarantee equality of civil, political, and religious rights. The last condition was aimed at forcing Romania to repeal its laws discriminating against Jews.

Jews first began immigrating to Romania in substantial numbers after 1829. From 1859 to 1899, the number of Jews in Moldavia increased from about 118,000 to 200,000, while in Walachia it grew from 9,000 to

68,000. (In Iași, the Moldavian capital, about half the population was Jewish.) Fearing their rumored expertise in financial and business matters—areas that most Romanians remained ignorant of—the government passed laws preventing Jews from owning land or even becoming innkeepers. An article in the new constitution specifically forbade them from holding the civil and political rights of Romanian citizens.

This official anti-Semitism, which was to plague Romania over the course of the next century, was widely shared at all levels of Romanian society. The peasantry came to resent the Jewish role as moneylenders (a position they filled by default, as Romanian banks showed no interest in lending to the poor) and as stewards of large rural estates, which they managed on behalf of absentee landlords. The growing middle class viewed the Jews as competitors. And members of the rich landlord class that dominated the government, who themselves owed large sums to Jewish lenders, feared that if Jews were granted equal rights they would be in a position to simply buy out their clients.

The church at Curtea de Arges in Wallachia, originally built in the early 16th century, includes the tombs of King Carol I, King Ferdinand I, and their queens. (Courtesy Free Library of Philadelphia)

And so, in times of trouble, the Jewish minority became a scapegoat for the country's problems. In one historian's words, "The Romanians learned to curse the Turk, the Russian, the Hungarian . . . and to beat the Jew."

For all these reasons, Romania at first resisted the demands of the Congress of Berlin, as debate raged in the parliament and anti-Jewish protests erupted in the streets. But the European powers held firm, and eventually the government agreed to repeal most of the anti-Jewish statutes, although the changes left numerous loopholes that allowed continued discrimination. Nevertheless, the Great Powers signaled their satisfaction with the reforms, and in early 1881 they officially recognized Romania's independence.

In March 1881, the country's parliament proclaimed the "Kingdom of Romania." On May 22, amid much solemn fanfare in Bucharest's cathedral, Prince Carol was invested as King Carol I. The crown placed on his head at the ceremony had been fashioned from the metal of a Turkish cannon captured at the pivotal battle of Plevna.

The coronation was an expensive, glittering affair, and in some ways it showed how far the country had come in the 15 years since Carol arrived and found pigs rooting outside his "palace." (Carol responded to the squalor by building over the years a succession of expensive palaces that were "turreted, pinnacled and ornamented down to the last square meter.")

But not all the changes were so superficial. Romania borrowed heavily from abroad (primarily from Germany) to finance economic development, and by the end of the 19th century the country had nearly 9,000 miles of roadway and 2,000 miles of railroad (14,000 km and 3,100 km, respectively). Walachia began pumping petroleum from its own wells, and public schools were built throughout the country. Between 1870 and 1898, the kingdom's foreign trade more than tripled.

Peasant Revolt and the Balkan Wars

Most of this economic development, however, benefited only Romania's wealthy classes, while the vast majority of the country's peasantry continued to labor in debt and peonage. A peasant uprising in Walachia after the harsh winter of 1887–88 resulted in the government's passage of an agrarian reform act that proved as inadequate as those before it. The pressure in the countryside built up steadily over the next two decades until it exploded with unprecedented ferocity in 1907.

The peasant revolt that erupted in Moldavia in March of that year began as an anti-Semitic pogrom, or organized massacre, with mobs attacking Jewish middlemen. It rapidly spread through much of the country and took on the characteristics of full-fledged class warfare as the enraged peasantry sacked large rural estates, burned the mansions of the rich, and finally tried to march on Bucharest. The government declared a state of siege and brought out the army, which suppressed the revolt with brutal efficiency. The rebels, armed only with primitive weapons, stood no chance against modern firearms, and at least 11,000 peasants were killed.

Romania's political and economic elite was chilled by the paroxysm of violence, and under the leadership of the Liberal Party a land reform program more thorough than any previous program was enacted. It established a minimum wage for agricultural laborers, set a maximum rent that could be charged to peasants leasing land, created rural banks, and dispersed some 4 million hectares (10 million acres) to needy peasants. Although it did not attack the root causes of the land conflict, the program was a positive step that temporarily helped reduce social tensions.

As a small, vulnerable state in a volatile region, Romania cast about for allies to help protect it against potential enemies. In 1883, King Carol had signed a secret treaty of alliance with Germany and Austria-Hungary—the so-called Central Powers. The treaty was a product of Romania's abiding mistrust of Russia, combined with the weakened power of France, Romania's traditional ally, and Carol's predilection toward his own German heritage.

The treaty was so secret that the only copy of it was kept locked inside the king's personal safe in the mountain castle that served as his summer retreat. The parliament had no idea of its existence. In some Romanian governments, Carol was the *only* person who was aware of the vital document. When the treaty came up for renewal in later years, certain key ministers were "brought into the loop."

One reason for the secrecy was to avoid antagonizing Britain, France, and Russia, who later joined together to form the Triple Entente, set up to counter the Central Powers. But a more important one was to avoid outraging the Romanian people themselves. It was clear to all concerned that Romanians would be horrified to discover they were formally allied with Austria-Hungary, the power that occupied Bukovina and Transylvania.

The issue was particularly sensitive because, during the period from 1879 to 1910, the Hungarian authorities enacted increasingly draconian laws to oppress non-Magyar nationalities in Transylvania. The use of the Hungarian language was mandated in schools, a campaign was launched to Magyarize family names, and when the Romanian masses tried to protest and organize politically, they were arrested and their rights of assembly were abolished. All of this sparked public outrage in Romania, along with calls for unification with Transylvania.

The international situation became almost impossibly complicated in 1912–13, the period of the two Balkan Wars. Austria-Hungary was becoming extremely concerned with the threat posed by Serbia, and began to see Bulgaria as a potential ally. This worried Romania, which had territorial conflicts with Bulgaria. Then, in the First Balkan War of October 1912, Bulgaria joined with Serbia, Montenegro, and Greece to attack the waning Ottoman Empire, with the tacit approval of Russia. Romania sat on the sidelines as the Balkan states dealt the Turks a serious defeat. In the negotiations that followed, Romania and Bulgaria quarreled bitterly.

The Second Balkan War erupted in June 1913 when Bulgaria, emboldened by its successes, turned on its former allies and attacked Serbia and Greece. In a bizarre shift of alliances, this time both Romania and Turkey joined in the fighting against Bulgaria, which had seriously overestimated its own strength. The brief war ended with Romania in control of the southern Dobruja region that had previously been part of Bulgaria. But the Balkans remained dangerous, and the stage was now set for the cataclysmic struggle initially called the Great War, although it ultimately became known as World War I.

World War I and Greater Romania

On June 28, 1914, a Bosnian Serb terrorist assassinated Austria's Archduke Franz Ferdinand in the Bosnian capital of Sarajevo, touching off a continent-wide conflict. Ferdinand, the heir to the Hapsburg throne, was the most prominent advocate in Austria-Hungary of the rights of Transylvania's Romanians. Austria issued a harsh ultimatum to Serbia, which was allied with Russia and France, that was tantamount to a declaration of war.

Initially, King Carol felt that since Austria had provoked Serbia with its ultimatum, the circumstances did not obligate Romania to honor its secret treaty with the Central Powers. But he swiftly became squeezed by both sides: The Central Powers appealed to his German heritage and promised that Romania would win back Bessarabia if it joined in the coming war against Russia. Moscow, in turn, raised the prospect that Romania could gain control of Transylvania if it joined the Triple Entente.

On August 3, 1914, as war broke out across Europe, a dramatic meeting of the Romanian Crown Council (consisting of both government and opposition party leaders) was held at the king's Carpathian palace in Sinaia. Carol insisted on siding with the Central Powers. But the council—many of whose members had learned about the king's secret, unconstitutional treaty for the first time—voted, with the exception of one minister, to remain neutral. They knew the Romanian people would not join any war alongside their Hungarian enemy and against France, their longtime friend.

"You cannot imagine," the king remarked after the meeting, "how bitter it is to find oneself isolated in a country of which one is not a native."

A disconsolate Carol died in his sleep on October 10, 1914, without having left a direct heir. Following arrangements made 25 years before, he was succeeded on the throne by his nephew, Ferdinand I (1914–27). Ferdinand was a considerably weaker and less politically astute ruler than his uncle. If it had not been for the traumatic outbreak of war, Carol's passing would have occasioned a much more emotional outburst of national mourning in Romania, for he had presided over the most peaceful and prosperous 48-year era in his adopted country's history.

Romania clung to its neutrality for the first two years of the war, and even profited handsomely by it, selling grain, oil, and other goods to both sides at inflated prices. Meanwhile, Bucharest engaged in extensive diplomatic haggling with both the Central Powers and the Triple Entente, seeking the best possible territorial deal before it entered the conflict on one side or the other. Ferdinand's wife, Queen Marie, was a member of both the British and Russian royal families and used her contacts to pass Romania's demands along to the governments of both countries.

In the summer of 1916 the battlefield situation seemed to be tipping toward the Entente, which finally agreed to Romania's conditions: that it would ultimately gain control of Transylvania, Bukovina, and the Banat from Austria-Hungary and perhaps even Bessarabia from Russia. The Crown Council met again on August 27, 1916, and declared war on Germany and Austria-Hungary. King Ferdinand, however, was traumatized by having to forsake his German roots. According to a French envoy, he appeared "ravaged by an interior struggle, his voice cut with sobs, his hands trembling."

The good news was that Romania had backed what ultimately proved to be the winning side in World War I. The bad news—typical of the country's tortured history—was that it would suffer terribly before finally reaping its reward. Romania's military establishment, previously dependent on German arms and advisers, was thoroughly unprepared for modern war. Britain and France initially could not deliver on their promises of military aid, and the Russian troops that entered Romania to lend support proved to be worse than useless, leaving all the hard fighting to their Romanian "allies."

The Romanian army invaded Transylvania, but was quickly driven back by German and Austrian forces, while the combined armies of Germany, Bulgaria, and Turkey counterattacked from the south. Bucharest and the rest of Walachia came under occupation as the Romanian government retreated to Moldavia. There, with the help of a French military mission, a reorganized Romanian army scored some successes on the battlefield. But with the triumph of the Bolshevik Revolution against Russia's provisional government in November 1917, Russia was transformed from a weak ally into an actively hostile power as the Bolsheviks made peace with Germany and withdrew from the war.

Now completely isolated, Romania sued for peace with the Central Powers. The terms were harsh: It ceded most of Transylvania to Hungary and Dobruja to Bulgaria, and was forced to sign its agricultural and oil wealth over to Germany while paying reparations to a German occupation army even as thousands of Romanians were dying from famine and disease. By the end of the war, Romania had suffered more than 800,000 military and civilian dead, a huge total for such a small country. The only positive development was that Romania gained control of Bessarabia from Russia.

But by the middle of 1918, aided by the American entry into the war against Germany, the military tide turned against the Central Powers. In November, Romania again declared war on Germany, and its army—which had not been demobilized—reoccupied Walachia and most of Transylvania. Nationalist assemblies in Transylvania, Bukovina, and Bessarabia voted for union with their Romanian motherland. In peace treaties signed in 1919 and 1920, the international community sanctioned virtually all of Romania's territorial claims, granting it sovereignty over Bessarabia, Bukovina, Transylvania, and Dobruja, and partitioning control of the Banat region between Romania and Serbia. Thus was Greater Romania born.

But the fighting was not quite over. In mid-1919, in response to provocations by a Communist regime led by Béla Kun, which briefly took power in Hungary, the Romanian army invaded Hungary and occupied its capital, Budapest. Taking what they saw as justified revenge for the looting of Romania during the war, the Romanian forces thoroughly plundered their historic enemy's territory. When they withdrew from Budapest in early 1920, under pressure from the western Allies, the Romanians took with them practically everything of value they could transport: railroad cars and locomotives, trucks, factory equipment, and food. After centuries of Hungarian domination over Romanians, this reversal of fortune further hardened attitudes between the two nations.

The Inter-War Years

Virtually overnight, Romania had more than doubled both its prewar population (from 7.5 million to 16 million) and territory (from about 86,000 square miles to 185,000 square miles [138,000 to 295,000 square km]). Although the expanded borders realized the age-old dream of uniting virtually all Romanians in one single state, they also brought in a much greater number of restive, non-Romanian nationalities. Whereas Romanians had made up 92 percent of the population in the old kingdom, that figure dropped to 70 percent in Greater Romania.

To ward off the prospect of revolution, and to keep patriotic promises made to the peasantry by King Ferdinand during the war, Romania's postwar governments enacted a series of political and social reforms. A new constitution in 1923 established Romania as a modern parliamentary monarchy with a highly centralized administration. Although the charter included a long list of guaranteed civil and political rights (such as universal male suffrage and citizenship for Jews), those rights were often more theoretical than real.

New agrarian laws passed between 1917 and 1921 substantially altered the country's system of land distribution. Huge swaths of land belonging to the boyars, the church, the Crown, and absentee landlords were sold to peasants to the point where small farmers with plots of 10 hectares (25 acres) or less now controlled more than 60 percent of the tilled land. But, as in previous land reform schemes, the small size of the plots—combined with corruption, lawsuits, insufficient rural credit, and inadequate farming equipment—meant that most peasants were still unable to escape their age-old cycle of poverty.

Although it remained a primarily agrarian country, Romania had considerable success in modernizing its industry during this period. Its industrial output doubled between 1923 and 1938, and by the mid-1930s it ranked second in Europe and seventh in the world in petroleum production. Its per capita income in 1938 was $94 (as compared to $81 in Portugal and $76 in Greece), although most of the wealth remained in the hands of the elite.

On the political scene, the old Conservative Party had been demolished by both the war, when it backed Germany, and the subsequent land reform, which lessened the power of its boyar patrons. Its traditional opponent, the Liberal Party, had by now strayed far from its populist 19th-century roots and was dominated by the country's industrial and financial classes. Its place on the political left was taken by the National Party (the major Romanian party in prewar Transylvania), which joined in 1926 with the old kingdom's Peasant Party to form the National Peasant Party. The Liberals retained power through mostly crooked elections from 1922 to 1928, while the National Peasant Party controlled the government, with one interruption, from 1928 to 1933.

A crisis in the royal family deepened Romania's continuing political turmoil. Crown Prince Carol II, Ferdinand's son and heir, was a notorious womanizer who married a Greek princess in 1921 but then promptly began a long-term affair with a divorced Jewish stenographer named

Elena (Magda) Lupescu. The highly publicized scandal made Romania the butt of jokes all over Europe. When King Ferdinand demanded his son break off the affair, Carol instead abdicated his right of succession and went into exile in Paris with Lupescu. Ferdinand died on July 19, 1927, and Carol's six-year-old son Michael was named king while a regency council ruled in his name.

Public dissatisfaction with the regency mounted when Romania was plunged into economic crisis by the Great Depression, the global economic crash that began in 1929. National Party Premier Iuliu Maniu agreed to allow Carol to return in 1930 if he broke off his affair, reconciled with his wife (they had been divorced in 1928), and agreed to rule initially only as co-regent, not king. Carol promptly broke all his promises, bringing Lupescu with him and allowing parliament to proclaim him King Carol II (1930–40). Maniu resigned in disgust. "Clever, tireless and quite without scruples he was exactly the king Romania did not need, for his own bad qualities matched and then magnified those of his country," as one modern writer has noted.

In the years that followed, Carol gradually revealed himself to be more of a royal dictator than a democratic monarch. To aid his consolidation of power, he forged informal and ambiguous links with the Iron Guard, an extreme nationalist, far-right, anti-Semitic, and anticommunist—that is to say, Fascist—group founded in the 1920s by Corneilu Zelea Codreanu. Codreanu was subsidized by Romanian industrialists who opposed the multiparty political system. The Iron Guard also received backing from abroad: first from the Fascist Party of Italian dictator Benito Mussolini and later from the Nazi Party of German dictator Adolf Hitler.

The Guard's official name was the Legion of the Archangel Michael, and its fanatical members were known as legionnaires. Jackbooted and wearing green shirts with little bags of "sacred" Romanian soil hanging from their necks, they assaulted leftists and Jews and engaged in political terrorism, assassinating premiers in 1933 and 1939. Poor, angry peasants flocked to the Iron Guard's banner, swelling its ranks until it became the largest Fascist party in the Balkans.

Carol eventually felt threatened by the Guard's power, and was shocked when its candidates won major victories in the 1937 elections. In 1938, the king cracked down on the legionnaires, arresting thousands of them. Codreanu and 13 other senior leaders were gunned down in prison "while trying to escape," although reportedly they were executed on Carol's orders. The king also suspended the constitution and proclaimed a royal dictatorship, ruling through the semi-Fascist "Front of National Renaissance" that he founded as a less extreme alternative to the Iron Guard.

Meanwhile, war again threatened Europe. Earlier, Romania had tried to design a system of international alliances to protect the gains it had made in World War I. In the 1920s, it had joined in a pro-French, anti-German pact with Czechoslovakia and Yugoslavia (two states that had emerged from the collapse of the Hapsburg Empire) known as the Little Entente. In the early 1930s, Romania added an alliance with Greece, Turkey, and Yugoslavia—the Balkan Entente, aimed mainly against Bulgaria.

Romania's confidence in its security net began to wane throughout the 1930s, as fascism increased its grip, and the growing might of Nazi Germany asserted itself on the world stage. Germany deliberately increased its influence in Romania, paying higher prices for its grain and oil, to the point where it accounted for half of Romania's total imports and exports. Hitler knew that Romania's agricultural and petroleum resources would be crucial to the German war machine in the coming war in Eastern Europe and Russia.

In September 1938, France and Britain signed the fateful Munich Agreement with Germany that allowed Hitler to carve up Czechoslovakia, making the Little Entente a dead letter. Feeling abandoned by her Western allies, Romania was forced to accommodate itself to German demands. In March 1939 the two countries signed a 10-year treaty of economic collaboration granting Germany extensive and exclusive rights to exploit Romania's natural resources.

World War II

In August 1939, Hitler signed a nonaggression pact with Soviet dictator Joseph Stalin, leaving Romania caught between the German and Russian juggernauts. The treaty freed Hitler to launch his invasion of Poland in September, starting World War II. Romania granted refuge and transit rights to the fleeing remnants of Poland's government and armed forces.

But, although Britain and France had previously guaranteed the independence of Romania, their quick defeats in the West at the hands of the Nazis made that bold pledge a hollow echo. British forces retreated to their home islands, and France surrendered in June 1940.

Unknown to Romania, the Nazi-Soviet pact had included a secret clause giving Moscow a free hand to reclaim Bessarabia. On June 26, 1940, the Soviets gave Romania a 24-hour ultimatum to turn over not only Bessarabia but also northern Bukovina, a region that had never been under Russian control. King Carol II, while trying to stay neutral in the conflict, was left with no choice but to give in to the Soviet demands. In August, under German, Soviet, and Italian pressure, Romania was forced to return southern Dobruja to Bulgaria and northern Transylvania to Hungary. Within three months, Greater Romania was swiftly dismembered, losing a third of its national territory and 4 million of its citizens.

This national humiliation proved to be the end for Carol. In a last-ditch effort to retain power, he named pro-legionnaire Marshal Ion Antonescu premier. But Antonescu, in league with the major political parties, army officers, and the Iron Guard, and with the full backing of Nazi Germany, forced Carol to abdicate on September 6, 1940. He fled into exile with Lupescu, his mistress, leaving his now 19-year-old son, Michael V (1940–47), to take the throne.

Antonescu assumed the grandiose title of Conducator, or leader (analogous to Hitler's *Führer*), ignored King Michael, and ruled as a military dictator in uneasy alliance with the Iron Guard. Beginning in October, German troops began moving into Romania, supposedly to "train" its armed forces and protect its vital oil industry. In reality, it was an army of occupation that eventually numbered up to one million men. On November 23, 1940, Romania officially joined the Nazi-led Axis Powers.

This period represented the high-water mark of the Iron Guard, which continued to function more as a macabre cult than a political movement. Nevertheless, it was tolerated by Antonescu and the cowed political elite. "In Legionnaire, bourgeois, nationalist Romania I saw the demon of sadism and stubborn stupidity incarnate before me," remarked playwright Eugène Ionesco.

In November 1940, Antonescu and the army stood by while the legionnaires launched a reign of terror, murdering Jews, kidnapping and killing Nicolae Iorga, a noted historian and one-time premier, and

New allies: Marshal Ion Antonescu and German field marshal Wilhelm Keitel at a 1941 parade in Bucharest celebrating the victory of Romanian troops over Soviet forces in Odessa. (Courtesy Library of Congress)

slaughtering 64 prominent members of King Carol's regime in Bucharest's central prison in revenge for the death of Codreanu. Finally, Germany decided that its fellow fascists had gone too far—after having served the Nazis' ulterior purpose of destabilizing Romania—and German and Romanian troops began rounding up the gangs of thugs. "I don't need fanatics, I need a healthy Romanian army," Hitler told Antonescu.

When Antonescu moved against the Iron Guard's leadership in January 1941, purging his regime of its members, the legionnaires staged an open rebellion aimed at seizing power for themselves. After they carried out a particularly ghastly massacre and mutilation of nearly 200 Jewish civilians in a slaughterhouse, German and Romanian soldiers cracked down hard and crushed the Iron Guard after several weeks of fighting.

On June 22, 1941, Germany broke its pact with Moscow and launched a lightning invasion of the Soviet Union across a broad front in Eastern Europe. German and Romanian armies attacked from the southwest and, in short order, Romania gained back northern Bukovina and

THE ROMANIAN HOLOCAUST

There were 800,000 Jews in Romania in 1939, the third-largest Jewish population in Europe. By the end of the war, only 400,000 remained. Although the numbers killed were horrifying they were not as high as the number of Jews deported and killed by other countries under the Nazis, such as Poland and France, which allowed a very large percentage of their Jewish citizens to be annihilated. The Romanian authorities under Gen. Ion Antonescu resisted deporting "their" Jews to Nazi death camps. (However, Hungary's Nazi regime did deport or kill 120,000 of Transylvania's 150,000 Jews in 1944.) Instead, Romanian soldiers, police, and Iron Guards initially murdered tens of thousands of Jews in vicious pogroms in Moldavia, Bukovina, and Bessarabia, as well as in the Ukrainian cities they conquered with their German allies, and later allowed hundreds of thousands of others to perish of disease and starvation.

But their crude methods were not as efficient as those perfected by the Germans, with their poison gas and crematoria. When told of the undisciplined massacre of 7,000 Jews carried out in a single night in June 1941 in Iaşi, Moldavia, by Romanian soldiers and civilians, one Nazi official commented disdainfully: "Pogroms are a Slavic specialty. In all things, we Germans are guided by reason and method and not by bestial instincts; we always act scientifically . . . We use surgeons, not butchers."

Labeling them all closet Bolsheviks (Communists), Antonescu's regime herded virtually the entire Jewish population of Bukovina and Bessarabia across the Dniester River into a desolate corner of the southwest Ukraine temporarily awarded to Romania by the Germans and dubbed "Transnistria." There, between 100,000 and 200,000 Jews were forced into concentration camps where up to three-quarters of them would die slowly of exposure, sickness, and hunger by the end of the war.

There was a ray of light amid the desolation, however. Siegfried Jagendorf, a Jewish engineer, persuaded the local Romanian authorities to allow him to repair a war-shattered foundry (ironworks factory) in the city of Moghilev. He recruited Jews as workers and devised projects to keep them alive and protect their wives, children, and the community's orphans. His heroic achievement, which ultimately saved up to 15,000 lives, bore a striking resemblance to the more famous effort of German industrialist Oskar Schindler, as chronicled in the book and movie *Schindler's List*.

Bessarabia from Soviet control. Many prudent Romanians felt they should have stopped there and left further conquests to the Germans. But with Antonescu calling for a "holy war" against communism, Romanian troops advanced across the Dniester River into the Ukraine with their German allies, seizing the Black Sea ports of Odessa and Sevastopol.

According to Grigore Gafencu, an intellectual Romanian statesman of the period, his country "was carried along in the vortex of the war, chained to a cause which was beyond her interest, fearing her ally as much as her adversary and the peace of tomorrow as much as the war of today."

Romania contributed more combat troops to the German war effort than all of the other Nazi allies combined. In part, it hoped to curry Hitler's favor so that Romania would win back northern Transylvania from Hungary after the war, which was expected to end in a quick victory for the Axis powers. But the German and Romanian columns became stalled on the frozen Russian steppes as one bitter winter passed, and then another. Finally, the turning point of the war was reached in the epic battle of Stalingrad, when the Soviet Red Army counterattacked and, in February 1943, totally destroyed the German and Romanian armies besieging the city.

It became increasingly clear that Germany would eventually lose the war. From the middle of 1943 on, acting separately, both the Antonescu regime and the leaders of Romania's opposition parties initiated secret negotiations with the Western Allies, even as British and American bombers were pounding Romanian factories and the oil fields at Ploiesti. Romania was ready to surrender to Anglo-American forces to avoid Soviet occupation, but the Western powers were unwilling to agree to a peace that excluded their Soviet ally.

In August 1944, the Red Army crossed into Moldavia. On August 23, King Michael, acting in concert with a coalition of opposition politicians, army officers, and Communist militiamen, staged a coup. Michael personally arrested Antonescu, announced the formation of a government of national unity, declared peace with the Allies, and demanded the withdrawal of German troops from Romania. The next day the German units, under orders from an enraged Hitler, began a savage bombardment of Bucharest in a failed attempt to crush the coup.

Soviet troops occupied Bucharest a week after Michael staged his patriotic putsch. They would subsequently serve as the shield behind which the tiny Romanian Communist Party, founded in 1921, would rise up and seize absolute power. To cover up their embarrassing lack of underground activity against the Germans to that point, the Communists claimed to have played the predominant role in overthrowing Antonescu, although more objective observers agreed that most of the credit belonged to Michael. It was not the last time the Communists would rewrite Romania's history to suit their purposes.

On September 12, Romania signed a treaty in Moscow requiring it to cede Bessarabia and northern Bukovina back to the Soviet Union and pay stiff reparations. Meanwhile, the Romanian army threw itself into the war against its former German allies with great vigor. In the first phase of the war against the Soviet Union, Romania had suffered several hundred thousand dead, missing, or captured (few prisoners returned alive from Soviet camps). In the last phase, fighting alongside the Red Army to liberate Hungary and Czechoslovakia, at least another 120,000 Romanians died. Altogether, Romania lost more men than the United States in all theaters of World War II, although it had only a small fraction of America's population.

NOTES

p. 29 "'Do not let France cool toward us . . .'" Denise Basdevant, *Against Tide and Tempest*, p. 62.

p. 31 "'Looking at the building . . .'" Hannah Pakula, *Queen Marie of Romania*, p. 36.

p. 34 "'The Romanians learned to curse the Turk . . .'" Siegfried Jagendorf, *Jagendorf's Foundry*, p. xix.

p. 34 "'turreted, pinnacled and ornamented . . .'" Pakula, op. cit., p. 39.

p. 37 "'You cannot imagine . . .'" Edward Behr, *Kiss the Hand You Cannot Bite*, p. 43.

p. 38 "'ravaged by an interior struggle . . .'" Behr, p. 44.

p. 41 "'Clever, tireless and quite without scruples . . .'" Mark Frankland, *The Patriots' Revolution*, p. 8.

p. 43 "'In Legionnaire, bourgeois, nationalist Romania . . .'" Norman Manea, *On Clowns: The Dictator and the Artist*, p. 3.

p. 44 "'I don't need fanatics, I need a healthy Romanian army.'" Jagendorf, p. xxii.

p. 45 "'Pogroms are a Slavic specialty. . . .'" Jagendorf, p. xxiv.

p. 45 "Siegfried Jagendorf, a Jewish engineer, . . ." Jagendorf, p. xxiv.

p. 46 "'was carried along in the vortex of the war . . .'" Basdevant, p. 104.

4

The Socialist Republic: Communism and Ceauşescu

For the next 35 years, the history of Romania would, in essence, be the history of its Communist Party. This was a remarkable development for a party that, at the end of World War II, listed fewer than 1,000 members on its official roll. "No East European communist movement had been as pathetically weak and unsuccessful before it came to power as the Romanian," one scholar has noted. If not for the strength of the Soviet Union and the wishes of its dictator, Joseph Stalin—and the relative weakness and indifference of the Western Allies—Romania's Communists might have remained a fringe party and its postwar history would have followed a very different course.

Following the anti-German coup of August 1944, King Michael appointed a coalition government dominated by the National Peasant and Liberal parties. It included as minister of justice Lucretiu Patrascanu, who became the first Communist to hold a high-level post in Romanian government. Iuliu Maniu's National Peasants called for quick national elections, but were stymied by the Communists and their Soviet backers, who knew they stood no chance in a fair vote. Instead, the Communists agitated against the coalition government until it fell in late 1944.

Michael next named a pro-Western general, Nicolae Radescu, as premier. In a nod to the Communists, Radescu appointed one of their senior leaders, Teohari Georgescu, as undersecretary of the interior ministry, from which position he was able to insert fellow party members into key posts in the police and security forces. Meanwhile, the Communists stepped up their campaign to seize power completely, vilifying Radescu, shutting down newspapers, and using squads of goons to assault political opponents in the streets and stir up trouble.

In late February 1945, with chaos in the streets and Soviet tanks ringing the palace, Moscow issued an ultimatum to the king: Replace Radescu with Petru Groza, leader of the pro-Communist Plowmen's Front, or risk the possibility of an outright Soviet takeover. As an added inducement, the Russians promised that Romania would regain permanent control of Transylvania. With the West showing no support, Michael had little choice but to consent.

Groza became premier on March 6, 1945, a date that in many ways marks the real Communist seizure of power in Romania. Although it was nominally a coalition government—with discredited, dissident members of the National Peasant and Liberal parties in the cabinet—it was in fact a Communist regime in all but name. Groza appointed Communists to head the army as well as the interior, economic affairs, justice, and propaganda ministries. As one Communist leader put it, the new regime had the effect of "detaching Romania from the imperialist camp." At Soviet urging, the government tried and executed Marshal Ion Antonescu and other senior members of his regime as war criminals in May and June.

Romania's postwar fate as a Soviet satellite had been secretly set at an October 1944 meeting in Moscow between Stalin and Prime Minister Winston Churchill of Great Britain. Churchill informally agreed that the Soviet Union could exercise 90 percent control in Romania in exchange for Britain being granted a similar free rein in Greece. Subsequent international conferences with the two leaders and President Franklin D. Roosevelt of the United States at Yalta in February 1945 and at Potsdam in the summer of that year did not recognize the prior agreement, but Stalin was to use it as justification for all subsequent Soviet actions in Romania.

The "Elections" of 1946 and 1948

The Romanian Communist Party (RCP) conducted an intense recruitment drive to build up its paltry numbers. From a mere 1,000 at war's end, the party swelled to more than 800,000 members by 1948 as many Romanians, clearly seeing which way the political wind was blowing, flocked to its banner. These new members included opportunists of all stripes, such as many ex-legionnaires of the fascist Iron Guard, whose politics theoretically were at the opposite end of the political spectrum from communism.

Meanwhile, the Communist leadership remained split between two main factions: the "home" Communists and the "Muscovites." The home Communists were native Romanians who mostly rose out of the labor movement and who had continued to operate underground in Romania during the war. Their leader was Gheorghe Gheorghiu-Dej, who had served a 12-year prison sentence after orchestrating a railroad strike in 1933. The Muscovites were Soviet-trained intellectuals, mostly nonethnic Romanians, who sat out the war in Moscow and returned to Bucharest with the Red Army. Their top leaders were Ana Pauker, a Moldavian Jew, and Vasile Luca, a Szekler from Transylvania who became a Soviet army major.

The two rival groups agreed to a wary, joint leadership at the Communist Party's first annual conference in October 1945. Stalin naturally favored the Muscovites, who controlled most of the actual levers of power, but he consented to Gheorghiu-Dej's appointment as general secretary. The Soviets realized the need to grant the home Communists a role because most Romanians did not trust the Muscovites, regarding them as foreign interlopers in thrall to Stalin. (In particular, their backing for returning Bessarabia to the Soviet Union struck most Romanian nationalists as treachery.)

After months of Communist strong-arm tactics against the political opposition, Romanians voted in the promised national elections in November 1946. In balloting widely seen as fraudulent, the Communists and their leftist party allies claimed 90 percent of the vote and 379 of the 414 seats in the National Assembly. The Western Allies went on in February 1947 to sign a final peace treaty with Romania that formally recognized the country's current boundaries. The treaty also obliged Romania to respect political freedoms and human rights, commitments that the Groza regime promptly ignored.

The cold war began in earnest in 1947 as the U.S.-led Western nations came to view Soviet actions in Eastern Europe as an aggressive threat to world peace. Stalin responded to the increased international tensions by ordering the Communists in the satellite states to seize complete power and toe Moscow's line on all matters. The obedient Romanian Communist Party launched a reign of terror against all its real and perceived political opponents, executing thousands and banishing the remainder to prison and work camps. National Peasant Party leader Iuliu Maniu, the most respected Romanian politician of his time, was given a life sentence on trumped-up charges of treason. He died in prison some years later.

In December 1947, Groza and Gheorghiu-Dej ordered King Michael to abdicate and leave the country or face civil war. He resisted as long as he could, but finally relented and went into exile in Switzerland. On December 30, the People's Republic of Romania was proclaimed.

Speaking of the docile Romanian people, Gheorghiu-Dej is reported to have cynically remarked: "Yesterday they were told to love the king, and they loved him. Today they are told to love us, and they will."

Love, hate, or indifference—Romanians were given no real choice in the matter. The Communists joined with one wing of the Social Democratic Party to form the Romanian Workers' Party and, in March 1948, held the last elections that included the pretense of an opposition. The Communist-led Popular Democratic Front won 405 of the 414 seats.

In April, the National Assembly adopted a new constitution. Although on paper the assembly was the supreme structure of the state, in reality, the Communists, unmentioned in the document, ruled the country as a supragovernmental entity through the Politburo and the Council of Ministers. The constitution contained the usual meaningless provisions of political and civil rights and even "guaranteed" the right to own private property—except where the "general interest" dictated otherwise. That handy clause was invoked to nationalize the country's entire financial, banking, insurance, transportation, industrial, and mining enterprises in the months and years that followed.

The Department of State Security, known as the Securitate, was established and began its long history of surveillance and repression of all facets of Romanian society. The Orthodox Church came under government control, other religions were persecuted, Western influence was suppressed in favor of Slavic culture, Russian-language instruction was made mandatory, and the national history was rewritten to stress the Soviet Union's "glorious" role in Romania's "liberation."

On the economic front, the regime followed the pattern of other Soviet satellite states of Eastern Europe. Romania's agricultural system was forcibly collectivized from 1948 to 1962, as peasants were pushed to give up their private plots and work on large state-owned farms. Some 80,000 peasants who resisted the process were arrested as "class enemies." The program resulted in food shortages and drove many farmers out of rural areas in search of jobs in urban centers. Meanwhile, in common with other Stalinist economies, the regime's Five-Year Plans put most of its resources into developing heavy industry, such as steel-making, petrochemicals, and vast construction projects like the Danube-Black Sea Canal.

The Gheorghiu-Dej Years

It is widely agreed among historians and independent experts that the Soviet Union exploited Romania—"plundered" might be a better word—more thoroughly and ruthlessly than any other Eastern European nation, with the possible exception of East Germany. In the immediate aftermath of the war, the Soviets looted the Romanian economy of as much as $2 billion in factory equipment, shipping, railroad stock, and manufactured goods, carting it all back to Russia. In the years that followed, the Soviets also required Romania to continue paying stiff war reparations and to help defray the costs of the presence of Soviet troops in the country.

The Soviets ran Romania like a profit-making machine, for that is what it represented to them. Romania received only a small fraction of the investment loans and credits that Moscow granted to its other satellite nations. In 1949, Romania joined the Council for Mutual Economic Assistance (CMEA), more commonly known as Comecon. It was set up by the Soviet Union to foster economic cooperation and integration among its East European allies, mostly to Moscow's benefit. Like Germany before, the Soviet Union and the other more highly industrialized

Communist leader Gheorghe Gheorghiu-Dej, left, and Stefan Voitech, vice president of the council of ministers, at a 1960 meeting of the UN General Assembly.
(AP Photos)

Comecon members saw Romania as a specialized source of food products and raw materials for the rest of the Eastern bloc, and so the Romanians were actively discouraged from developing their own heavy industry at the expense of agriculture.

Although Gheorghiu-Dej was himself a Stalinist at heart, he was a Stalinist for Romania, not Russia. He wanted to use the state's unchecked power to develop Romania's economy for its own people. In the parlance of the times, he was a "national Communist." But he had to keep his intentions under wraps because in the years after the 1948 Yugoslav-Soviet split (when Yugoslav leader Josip Broz, known as Marshal Tito, successfully broke away from Moscow's orbit) there were Stalin-inspired purges throughout the other satellite states of anyone who followed Tito's nationalist approach.

Stalin died in 1953. When Stalin's successor, Nikita Khrushchev, denounced him in 1956, Gheorghiu-Dej (although himself an ardent Stalinist) used Romania's ousted Muscovite faction as scapegoats for the earlier "excesses" of Romanian Communist rule. (Gheorghiu-Dej had purged the faction from the government in 1952.) Romania joined the Soviet-led Warsaw Pact military alliance in 1955, and backed the 1956 Soviet invasion that crushed Hungary's popular anticommunist revolution. But at the same time, Gheorghiu-Dej moved Romania onto an independent international course, pledging cooperation with any state, whether Communist or capitalist, so long as it respected Romania's sovereignty and did not meddle in its internal affairs. This stance led Romania to closer ties with Communist China, ruled by Mao Zedong, which advocated a similar course.

With Chinese backing, Gheorghiu-Dej craftily convinced Khrushchev to remove Soviet troops from Romania in 1957. Then, as the Sino-Soviet split came into the open in the late 1950s and early '60s, Romania was emboldened to increase its defiance of Moscow's dictates. While not throwing itself completely into the Chinese camp (as Albania did), Romania trod a delicate middle ground in the conflict. As one scholar subsequently noted: "On the overt basic issues of the Sino-Soviet dispute, [Gheorghiu-Dej] was always pro-Soviet; there was virtually no danger of his ever becoming a Maoist. Mao, to him, became simply a means of winning concessions from the Soviet Union."

Under Gheorghiu-Dej's leadership, Romania took a number of increasingly bold steps: It forged ties with Tito's Yugoslavia, began soliciting credits from Western nations to finance Romania's industrial development, rebuffed Khrushchev's demands that it "integrate" its economy with Comecon (i.e., stress agriculture over industry), and commenced a "de-Russification" of Romanian politics and culture. These moves proved popular with the nationalistic Romanian people and were in line with Gheorghiu-Dej's goal: to replace Soviet backing for his regime with genuine popular support. Up until that point, "Moscow had protected its vassals from popular anger; now the people (and the West) should protect the regime from the fury of the Kremlin."

Romania's campaign climaxed with the issuing of a Central Committee declaration on April 26, 1964. This so-called "Declaration of Independence" defiantly announced to Moscow and the world Romania's intention to go its own way in its economic affairs and international relations. It criticized both sides in the Sino-Soviet dispute. And it declared the Romanian party's complete autonomy from Soviet control: "No one can decide what is and what is not correct for other countries and parties. There is not and cannot be a 'parent' party and a 'son' party, a 'superior' and a 'subordinate' party."

The Soviets could do nothing; Romania's carefully crafted provocations fell short of providing justification for a military invasion. Romania's position was further strengthened by the abrupt ouster of Khrushchev in October 1964 and the installation of a more cautious Soviet leadership.

Gheorghiu-Dej died on March 19, 1965, at the age of 64, having achieved many of the aims he set out for himself and his country. Although he had presided over a period of terrible repression and wrenching social and economic changes in the 1950s, by the end of his life he had gained considerable respect both abroad and at home as a Romanian patriot.

He was succeeded by a triumvirate: Nicolae Ceauşescu as party leader, Ion Gheorghe Maurer as premier, and Chivu Stoica as state council president. But it was Ceauşescu who would quickly emerge on top, a position he would not relinquish until he had taken his country down a long road to ruin that reached its end with his violent overthrow nearly a quarter-century later.

The future dictator was only 47 when he was named first secretary of the Romanian Workers Party, but he had already been a Central Committee member for 13 years and a full Politburo member for 10. He had risen rapidly through the ranks due to his unswerving loyalty to Gheorghiu-Dej, whom he had met in prison during the war. He got along well with the working-class Gheorghiu-Dej: "The young Romanian peasant from the impoverished Olt valley who had become a Communist while still a teenager made a perfect acolyte; he was quick and shrewd, and had no tiresome pretensions to being an intellectual."

Romanian dictator Nicolae Ceauşescu in 1978 during a state visit to the United States. (Courtesy Jimmy Carter Library)

Ceauşescu's Consolidation of Power

Yet another Romanian constitution was adopted in 1965, after Gheorghiu-Dej's death. This nationalist document omitted all references to the Soviet Union and proclaimed that Romania was now a full-fledged "Socialist Republic" rather than merely a People's Republic, meaning the country had reached the final stage of development in Communist dogma. Underlining this supposed achievement, the Romanian Workers Party reverted to its previous name, the Romanian Communist Party.

The new leadership moved to demythologize Gheorghiu-Dej, criticizing his Stalinist policies and eradicating the "cult of personality" (emphasis on his personal greatness) that had been erected around him. There was little suspicion among his comrades that Ceauşescu himself would soon build a similar cult around his own person that would make Gheorghiu-Dej seem positively modest by comparison.

Some of the Communist old guard probably hoped that they could control Ceauşescu and keep him from gaining too much personal power. If so, they were to be sorely disappointed. He gradually eliminated all his major rivals and gained control of various key posts, including supreme military commander and state council president, while installing loyal followers in positions beneath him. By the time the Communist Party held its 10th party conference in 1969, Ceauşescu exercised nearly absolute control over his regime.

In the initial years of his reign, Ceauşescu traveled tirelessly around the country giving speeches to the masses, portraying himself as a Romanian nationalist and man of the people. The long-suffering population was given hope by his promises of loosened social controls, the rehabilitation of the reputations of some of Gheorghiu-Dej's political victims, and vows that the dreaded Securitate secret police would have to obey the rule of law.

Hopes were raised further as Ceauşescu pushed his predecessor's independent foreign policy to new heights. In 1967, Romania established diplomatic relations with West Germany and then maintained ties with Israel after the rest of the Eastern bloc broke their ties in the wake of Israel's victory over the Arabs in the Six Day War. The crowning moment came in 1968, when the forces of the Soviet-led Warsaw Pact invaded Czechoslovakia to crush the "Prague Spring" reformist government of Alexander Dubček. Ceaușescu openly condemned Moscow's aggression and refused the request for Romanian troops to join in the intervention.

For standing up to the Soviets, Ceaușescu won praise not only from the West—French president Charles de Gaulle visited Romania in 1968 and U.S. President Richard Nixon followed suit in 1969—but from the Romanian people as well. Intellectuals and artists flocked to join the

---

CEAUȘESCU'S EARLY YEARS

The thick fog of mythology built up around Ceaușescu's early life by later Communist historians has begun to lift in recent years, creating a more accurate picture. He was born on January 26, 1918, in the Walachian village of Scornicesti, the third son of a small-time farmer. He moved to Bucharest as a teenager—in part to escape his drunken, violent father—and briefly became an apprentice to his uncle, a shoemaker. He developed a reputation as a hooligan and was arrested for street brawling before joining the Young Communists' League. "Nicolae got involved for the violence rather than for the ideology," according to one well-placed Romanian historian.

Certain exploits credited to him in his authorized biographies (such as his election to Romania's national anti-Fascist committee at the age of 15) were in fact attributable to his older brother Marin, who was subsequently kept out of the limelight to avoid embarrassing questions. A youthful contemporary of Nicolae recalls him as someone "whom everyone despised . . . He was dull, physically unprepossessing, on the small side, and afflicted with a risible stammer, which was so bad people avoided him—they didn't want to laugh in his face," especially because he was prone to unpredictable rages.

Later, with the help of his wife Elena, whom he married in 1946 and who came to exercise great power over her husband, he conquered his stammer and became a passable public speaker. Both were poorly educated and harbored a lifelong distrust of intellectuals, although in their later years they were fulsomely celebrated as great thinkers and numerous books were ghost-written for them. In the view of a leading Romanian Communist, Silviu Brucan, Nicolae was "shrewd and smart," while Elena was "shrewd but stupid." Such words, of course, were uttered only after their deaths.

Wiretap gear of the dreaded Securitate secret police, who spied on all sectors of Romanian society. (AP/Wide World Photos)

Communist Party, believing that Ceauşescu was allowing his own version of a reformist "Bucharest Spring" to develop. They did not see the danger that a homegrown totalitarianism was on the horizon that would be just as bad as the Soviet variety. "We have been so preoccupied with the danger of Soviet occupation that for all practical purposes we have pre-occupied ourselves," one Romanian prophetically observed at the time.

Whatever his flaws, Ceauşescu was perceived as first and foremost a nationalist. The writer Paul Goma, one of the few dissidents who stood up to the regime in its later phase, noted that during those early years, "The general feeling was, among the vast majority of Romanians, Okay, he's a communist but at least he's against the Russians, the Hungarians, the Jews; he's one of *us*."

But the members of the intelligentsia that joined the party ultimately found it to be a trap. "It was easy to join the Party [but] almost impossible to leave it because that meant abandoning both social life and one's profession," a Bucharest literature professor has said. "An intellectual who left the Party had two choices, to emigrate, or to become marginalized."

So Ceaușescu's promise of a political, social, and cultural opening in the late 1960s proved to be ephemeral. For careful observers, the writing was already on the wall as early as 1966, when Ceaușescu first began implementing policies—such as restrictions on abortion, contraceptives, divorce, and emigration—that the West did not begin complaining about until the 1980s.

These policies grew in part out of Nicolae and Elena Ceaușescu's strong puritanical streak: They opposed sexuality, drinking, smoking, and frivolity in general. They launched campaigns against "decadent" Western practices of the 1960s, such as long hair, beards, and miniskirts, and rejected the West's concepts of political and artistic freedom. "The common denominator of our socialist art is the Marxist-Leninist ideal," Ceaușescu announced in 1968. In that same year he also proclaimed, "We do not understand democracy in its bourgeois meaning—of babbling, lack of discipline, anarchy. We understand democracy as the active participation of the citizens in formulating and implementing the Party's policy."

Similarly, rather than reining in the Securitate as he had pledged, he allowed the secret police to flourish like some poisonous, choking weed. "It has been said that a good political machine thrives on the visibility of its rewards and the certainty of its punishments," one historian has noted. "Ceaușescu's punishments were not ultimate—he killed only a few of his opponents—but they were certain: harassment, demotion, transfer, house arrest and prison. The Securitate penetrated deeply into the fabric of Romanian society, creating a pervasive atmosphere of fear by continually testing the loyalty of every citizen in the country and intimidating all but the most foolhardy."

By the 1970s it had become clear that Ceaușescu, a creative maverick in foreign affairs, was simply a small-minded tyrant at home. As one scholar put it in 1988, before the collapse of communism:

> In foreign policy the communists inherited and continued the best and most skillful characteristics of the old regime; in domestic policy they took over some of the worst and amplified them. Nationalist and resourceful in foreign policy, the Bucharest regime under Ceaușescu became tyrannical and unresourceful at home, with all

those characteristics of nepotism, corruption, and indifference to popular needs that had disfigured Romania's prewar governmental systems. Romania came to be considered the worst-governed East European country . . . What steadily developed in Romania during the 1970s can loosely be described as neo-Stalinism without terror. The result was creeping disintegration.

"Pharaonic" Socialism

A turning point in Ceauşescu's rule came when he and Elena visited the Far East in 1971, where they were deeply influenced by what they saw in Communist China and North Korea. In China under Mao Zedong, the Cultural Revolution—a violent, anti-intellectual purge aimed at eradicating all vestiges of capitalism and Western influence—was in full swing. Elena was apparently particularly impressed by the prominence and power being wielded by Mao's wife, Jiang Qing. The Ceauşescus were also fascinated by North Korean dictator Kim Il Sung and his penchant for glorifying his rule with massive building projects. They were enamored with his super-orderly capital, Pyongyang, with its wide, empty avenues and endless rows of identical apartment blocks.

The Ceauşescus would eventually transplant these modern versions of Oriental despotism back to their homeland, creating a monstrous cult of personality around themselves, "the sheer ludicrousness of which insulted, humiliated, angered or amused most Romanians." Thus commenced the period of what some observers have called "pharaonic socialism" (a reference to the pharaohs, the all-powerful god-kings of ancient Egypt who had the pyramids built as eternal monuments to their greatness). The process began when, on his return from Asia, Ceauşescu promulgated his "July theses," which called for a stringent discipline in cultural affairs.

The pharaonic phase, which grew steadily worse until the revolution of 1989, has also been characterized as "dynastic socialism," or rule by a family dynasty rather than the Communist Party. Increasingly suspicious, even paranoid, of his enemies, Ceauşescu in the late 1970s and early 1980s promoted unqualified but loyal family members—his wife, his son Nicu (who had a well-justified reputation as a "socialist playboy"), three of his brothers, and a brother-in-law—to influential posts in the

Volumes "written" by and about Ceauşescu dominate a Bucharest bookstore's window display in 1988. (AP/Wide World Photos)

ministries of science and technology, party cadres, youth, defense, and internal affairs.

Aside from family members, Ceauşescu surrounded himself with sycophants who agreed to everything he proposed, no matter how outrageous—a form of government that one scholar dubbed a "sycophantocracy." Elena became the most powerful woman in the Eastern bloc, joining the Politburo in 1973 and ultimately becoming first deputy premier. Despite her limited education, she claimed to be a world-class chemist and engineer. People were required to celebrate her as a so-called "eminent personage of Romanian and international science."

Still more fulsome praise was heaped on her husband. His dictatorship was referred to as the "Epoch of Light" and the "Golden Age." The list of his attributes was endless: He was "the Genius of the Carpathians," the "savior of the nation," the "hero of peace," the "most brilliant revolutionary thinker of all times," the "torchbearer among torchbearers," "unique as a mountain peak," and, despite his stammering, "our famous lullaby trill"—all of these qualities tempered by his "saintly modesty." Ceauşescu apparently came to believe that the huge crowds organized by party functionaries to applaud him wherever he went were genuine evidence of his popular adoration, when they were in fact "a permanent ceremonial enacted by the entire country in front of a single spectator."

Although they could not say so in public, most Romanians undoubtedly found this personality cult ridiculous. Nevertheless, if the eccentricities of Ceauşescu's rule had been restricted to phony accolades and grandiose monuments, his fellow countrymen could probably have learned to live with them. Much more damaging, however, were the drastic economic and social policies that he was able to implement due to his unchecked power. These could not be laughed off.

Following his primitive Stalinist instincts, Ceauşescu sought to underline Romania's national independence by pouring virtually all of the country's resources into heavy industry at the expense of agriculture, building high-risk, uneconomical steel mills, petrochemical plants, and shipyards, and restarting work on the monumental (and unnecessary) Danube-Black Sea canal. At first Romania was able to afford these projects thanks to an influx of loans from Western nations, especially after 1972 when it became the first Comecon country to join the International Monetary Fund (IMF) and World Bank.

For the first half of the 1970s, Romania actually seemed to be enjoying a period of prosperity, although it was a hollow one that could not last. As its own petroleum resources dwindled, it turned to importing oil from the Middle East, forging close relations with the Arab states and Iran. But as the price of oil skyrocketed in the mid-1970s, Romania's foreign debt rose accordingly, and by 1980 it owed $11 billion to the West. In 1981 Romania was on the verge of bankruptcy and became the second Comecon country (Poland was the first) to have to reschedule its debt payments to Western bankers.

In the early 1980s, in a typically idiosyncratic move that verged on economic lunacy, Ceauşescu launched a crash program to pay off all of Romania's foreign debts within a decade, declaring that interest payments to the West were equivalent to the tribute Romanians had previously paid to the Ottoman Empire. The regime cut domestic electricity usage, slashed imports and stepped up exports, particularly from the agricultural sector.

As a result, life for the vast majority of Romanians—never luxurious even in the best of times—became one of unrelieved misery. People were restricted to one 40 watt lightbulb per room, central heating plants kept wintertime temperatures in apartment complexes in the low 50s Fahrenheit (that is, when heat was available, sometimes only for a few hours a day), and hot water was frequently unavailable for weeks at a time.

Despite rationing, food was hard to come by for most people, as most of the country's agricultural wealth was being exported for hard currency. Showing how out of touch with reality he really was, Ceauşescu in 1982 accused his countrymen of being too fat and launched an effort to reduce Romanians' caloric intake through a "program of scientific nourishment." The Ceauşescus themselves sought to practice what they preached. They were "weight-watchers and food freaks. They were natural converts to organic food, as much on their guard against poisoning by impurities as by their enemies . . . When Ceauşescu said Romanians would do better to eat less it was not just the remark of a cynical dictator. He was offering a piece of royal wisdom. The ruling pair set an example by their own leanness."

While Romania became the "Ethiopia of Europe," the regime lied to itself and the world. In late 1989, shortly before he was overthrown, Ceauşescu announced a bumper grain harvest of 60 million tons, when the actual total was less than 17 million tons.

The Romanian people themselves were not deceived, but there was not much they could do about it. There were widespread protests by factory workers in 1987, but the demonstrations were quickly crushed with hundreds of arrests. (The regime had reacted similarly after one of the few earlier outbreaks of unrest, a strike by miners in the Jiu Valley region in 1977.)

As one observer has put it:

Ceauşescu had done what none of his Soviet-bloc colleagues dared: break the unwritten contract between Communists and the working class. Fearful of the consequences of admitting economic failure and the need for sacrifices, the other leaders had gone on borrowing in the West largely to keep living standards artificially high . . . Ceauşescu had the nerve to do what the other East European leaders were often tempted to but never dared: treat his working class as harshly as he thought they deserved.

The daily difficulty of huddling in cold, dark rooms, and scavenging for food was bad enough. Ceauşescu increased the misery index still further with various cruel social policies. One of the most notorious was his "pro-birth" program, a misguided effort to increase Romania's population by banning abortions and the sale of contraceptives. The policy was originally implemented in 1966 and was made still more intrusive in the 1980s when the regime actually began requiring monthly gynecological checkups of women at their workplaces to ensure that if a woman became pregnant she would be forced to carry her pregnancy to term.

This bizarre experiment in Orwellian Big Brotherhood backfired horribly. Far from permanently increasing the birth rate, by the mid-1980s the rate was back to where it had been in 1966. Its main effect was a huge increase in the death rate among pregnant women, which jumped from 86 deaths per 100,000 live births in 1966 to 150 in 1984, with most of the increase attributable to botched, illegal abortions. Many of the women who did give birth were too poor to care for their babies and were forced to abandon them. Thousands of infants (many of whom contracted the AIDS virus due to a widespread Romanian medical practice of unchecked blood transfusions) were warehoused in wretched state orphanages, a haunting legacy that will be explored in more detail in a later chapter.

The other, most glaring example of Ceauşescu's social engineering was his policy of "systemization" and "modernization" of the Romanian countryside. This "rural urbanization" program aimed at demolishing thousands of Romania's ancient and historic towns and villages—those considered "irrational" and "nonviable"—and moving their inhabitants against their will into poorly constructed suburban housing projects ("agro-industrial centers") where they would supposedly have greater access to government services.

The systemization strategy, originally developed in the 1970s, was further elaborated by Ceauşescu in the late 1980s. Fortunately for most Romanians, the cash-strapped regime did not have the resources to carry out the program on a large scale. Nevertheless, thousands of Romanians were forced to evacuate their homes and watch them get bulldozed, and many village churches were razed. The program also caused a major crisis in Romania's relations with Hungary in 1988. Many ethnic Hungarian villages in Transylvania were targeted for destruction, the latest step in Romania's longstanding effort to forcibly assimilate its Hungarian minority.

By this stage, Romania had succeeded in alienating itself from both the East and the West. Ceaușescu strongly resisted Soviet leader Mikhail Gorbachev's calls for reform, and the Bucharest regime came to be considered an embarrassment to the other more moderate East European Communist states. Meanwhile Western nations, after years of smiling upon Ceaușescu because of his independence from Moscow, finally grew weary of his unpredictable behavior and appalling human rights record. The United States was on the verge of revoking Romania's most favored

"The house that Ceaușescu built": The grandiose People's Palace, supposedly the second-largest building in the world, was opened to the public after the revolution. (Courtesy Romanian National Tourist Office, New York)

nation (MFN) trading status in 1988 when Ceauşescu himself preemptively renounced it.

There is one more aspect of Ceauşescu's misrule that deserves comment: He did not spare the Romanian capital from the destruction his policies had wrought in the countryside. Ever since returning from North Korea in 1971, he had longed to reproduce Pyongyang's sterile, monumental architecture in Bucharest. Damage from an earthquake in 1977 gave him the excuse to order the demolition to begin. Elaborate plans were laid, and in 1984 an entire city district housing 40,000 people—and including beautiful, historic architecture, churches, and a monastery—was leveled to clear the way for the Victory of Socialism Boulevard and a massive complex of government buildings.

The only structure that was nearly completed when Ceauşescu was ousted was the 6,000-room People's Palace, also known as the House of the Republic. It was meant to be the largest building in the world, although the Pentagon, which houses the U.S. Department of Defense in Washington, D.C., apparently still owns that honor. At a cost of untold millions of dollars, 17,000 men worked 24 hours a day on the project, guarded by Securitate agents and constantly supervised by Ceauşescu ("Dracula driving a bulldozer") and his wife. Today the People's Palace stands empty, a fitting epitaph to the "Epoch of Light."

Virtually all observers agree that, even if it is not the largest building in the world, it is certainly one of the ugliest. "Here, the Communist-pharaonic disease of gigantism reached its apogee" in a "monument to vandalism as well as megalomania."

Western students of Romanian history have had some difficulty coming to grips with Ceauşescuism. Romanian-born scholar Nestor Ratesh perhaps put it best when he wrote:

> Some intellectual endeavor was devoted to finding a formula that described the peculiarity of the Ceauşescu regime in the 1970s and 1980s. For some, it was a primitive Stalinism. Others added a touch of Byzantine tradition to the classical communist totalitarianism, and still others spoke of an ersatz society, a pseudo-neo-Stalinism. There might have been a bit of all these ingredients, although in the end it looked in many respects like pure madness.

NOTES

p. 49 "'No Eastern European communist movement . . .'" J. F. Brown, *Eastern Europe and Communist Rule*, p. 267.

p. 50 "'detaching Romania from the imperialist camp.'" Edward Behr, *Kiss the Hand You Cannot Bite*, p. 108.

p. 52 "'Yesterday they were told to love the king, . . .'" Behr, p. 108.

p. 55 "'On the overt basic issues . . .'" J. F. Brown, *The New Eastern Europe: The Khrushchev Era and After*, p. 206.

p. 55 "'Moscow had protected its vassals . . .'" Paul Lendvai, *Eagles in Cobwebs*, p. 301.

p. 55 "'No one can decide what is . . .'" Lendvai, p. 309.

p. 56 "'The young Romanian peasant . . .'" Mark Frankland, *The Patriots' Revolution*, p. 299.

p. 58 "'Nicolae got involved for the violence . . .'" Behr, p. 56.

p. 58 "'whom everyone despised . . .'" Behr, p. 57.

p. 58 "'shrewd and smart . . .'" Frankland, p. 312.

p. 59 "'We have been so preoccupied . . .'" Michael Shafir, *Romania—Politics, Economics and Society*, p. 150.

p. 59 "'The general feeling was, . . .'" Behr, p. 146.

pp. 59–60 "'An intellectual who left the Party . . .'" Frankland, p. 99.

p. 60 "'The common denominator of our socialist art . . .'" Behr, p. 147.

p. 60 "'Ceauşescu's punishments were not ultimate . . .'" Gale Stokes, *The Walls Came Tumbling Down*, p. 57.

pp. 60–61 "'In foreign policy the communists inherited . . .'" J. F. Brown, *Eastern Europe and Communist Rule*, p. 275.

p. 61 "'the sheer ludicrousness of which . . .'" Brown, p. 276.

p. 63 "'a permanent ceremonial enacted . . .'" Stokes, p. 54.

p. 64 "'weight-watchers and food freaks. . . .'" Frankland, p. 297.

p. 64 "'Ceauşescu had done what none of his Soviet-bloc colleagues dared: . . .'" Frankland, p. 306.

p. 67 "'Dracula driving a bulldozer." Behr, p. 219.

p. 67 "'Here, the Communist-pharaonic disease . . .'" Eva Hoffman, *Exit into History: A Journey Through the New Eastern Europe*, p. 308.

p. 67 "'monument to vandalism as well as megalomania.'" J. F. Brown, *Eastern Europe and Communist Rule*, p. 282.

p. 67 "'Some intellectual endeavor was devoted to . . .'" Nestor Ratesh, *Romania: The Entangled Revolution*, p. 3.

5

REVOLUTION

In 1989, with Communist regimes around Eastern Europe toppling like a row of dominoes, Romania stood alone. But even there, some of the first signs of overt dissent had begun to appear. Literature professor Doina Cornea and poets Mircea Dinescu and Anna Blandiana raised their voices in daring public protests. Three editors from *Romania Libera* (Free Romania), the country's second-largest official newspaper, were arrested when they attempted to publish an anti-Ceauşescu edition. (They were sentenced to death but were spared by the revolution.) Even the government's official representative to the United Nations Commission on Human Rights was placed under house arrest after he issued a report highly critical of the regime's abuses.

But the most significant development came in the spring of 1989 when a group of six leading Romanian Communists and former senior government officials sent Ceauşescu an open letter harshly criticizing his dictatorial rule. This famous "Letter of Six" was drafted by Marxist theoretician Silviu Brucan and signed by him and five others, including former foreign minister Corneliu Manescu, former party first secretary Gheorghe Apostol, and party founding member Constantin Pirvulescu, then 94 years old. The letter accused Ceauşescu of suspending the constitution, violating the 1975 Helsinki Accords on human rights (which Romania had signed), destroying Bucharest in the name of rebuilding it, wrecking the economy and agriculture, and indulging in "harebrained schemes" to modernize the country.

Ceauşescu ignored the letter and had its signers placed under house arrest or banished to internal exile. Nevertheless, it was widely publicized abroad and alerted Romanians to the fact that even veteran elements of the Communist establishment had lost all faith in their leader. The country seemed to hold its collective breath, waiting for something to happen, assuming someone else would start it, whatever *it* was. "It was like waiting for a train," a leading intellectual said. "You knew it would come, but you didn't know when."

As if nothing were amiss, the Romanian Communist Party went ahead with its 14th Party Conference in late November. Unanimously "reelected" president, Ceauşescu gave his usual six-hour speech, interrupted by "stormy applause," in which he criticized Romania's neighbors for not behaving like good socialists.

Plotters may indeed have been waiting in the wings, but a spark was needed to ignite the flimsy tinderbox that Ceauşescu's regime had become. That spark would flare in a most unlikely place.

The Timişoara Trigger

The place was Timişoara, a charming city in western Romania. Although some regard it as being in Transylvania, it is more accurately described as the capital of the Banat region, where for centuries Hungarians, Saxons, Serbians, and other, smaller ethnic minorities had lived peaceably alongside the Romanian majority. This ethnic harmony, unusual for Romania, was in fact a crucial element that helps explain the solidarity that Timişoara displayed in rising up against Ceauşescu in December 1989.

Since most Romanians regard Hungarians with suspicion, it is ironic that the trigger for the rebellion was a Hungarian Protestant pastor, Rev. Laszlo Tokes of the Reformed Church. He had become an irritant to the regime, publicly criticizing its abuses, especially the "systemization" program to destroy rural villages. Earlier in the year, he had been ordered to transfer from Timişoara to a remote village parish. When he refused to go, an embarrassed church hierarchy asked the government to evict him from his church.

On December 15, the deadline for eviction, a thousand people gathered in the square outside the church. Initially, they were mostly Hungarians, but they were quickly joined by Romanians, Serbs, and others. Clashes with police and militia broke out, but the deadline passed with Tokes unevicted. The next day the crowds swelled to as many as 10,000, joined by students and other young people, and the protests took on the character of a full-fledged anticommunist uprising. Shouts of "Down with Ceauşescu," "Down with the dictator," and "Today in Timişoara, tomorrow in the whole country" rang out in the streets. Troops were mobilized to stop the marchers, although there was no gunfire and there were no deaths (apparently most of the soldiers had been issued unloaded weapons). Late on the night of December 16, Securitate agents stormed the church and beat and arrested Tokes. But it was too late, for he had already served his purpose—the revolution had begun.

An enraged Ceauşescu, joined by his wife, Elena, called an emergency meeting of the party's Political Executive Committee December 17 in Bucharest. (The meeting was tape-recorded and a transcript was later released.) He ranted that the Timişoara uprising was a foreign plot, hatched in Washington and Moscow and carried out by Hungarian agents. He lambasted defense minister General Vasile Milea, interior minister Tudor Postelnicu, and the Securitate chief, General Iulian Vlad, for not arming the anti-riot troops with live ammunition to suppress the "hooligans."

"They should have fired to bring them down, to warn them, and then to fire at their legs . . . You don't put an enemy down with sermons, you have to burn him," Ceauşescu shouted. Elena pitched in: "You should have fired on them, and had they fallen, you should have taken them and shoved them into a cellar. Weren't you told that? Not one of them should have gotten out."

The committee then approved Ceauşescu's formal order to arm the troops in Timişoara and "wherever there is an attempt of [antigovernment] action, liquidate it radically, without a word." After the dictator made a false threat to resign, his aides fell to their knees and promised to carry out his orders. Mollified, and demonstrating a surreal sense of confidence totally unjustified by the circumstances, Ceauşescu left early the next morning for a long-planned three-day state visit to Iran.

December 17 was "Bloody Sunday" in Timişoara. Milea and Vlad were not among the anti-Ceauşescu plotters but they could see which way the wind was blowing and apparently had no intention of carrying out the dictator's bloodthirsty orders. Perhaps suspecting this, Ceauşescu had already dispatched a key aide, Ion Coman, to Timişoara to take command and carry out the shoot-to-kill policy. That evening, uniformed soldiers and plainclothes agents opened fire on the huge crowd gathered in the central square. The shooting continued for the next two days.

The actual death toll remains in dispute to this day. Initial reports in the foreign news media suggested that many thousands had died. It is possible that this was a deliberate exaggeration by the anti-Ceauşescu plotters in order to fan the flames of popular rebellion. The official count from the post-revolutionary government was around 100, and this may be closer to the truth. But whatever the total, it was clear that a major massacre had taken place. Romanians throughout the country heard about the bloodshed on shortwave radio from Radio Free Europe and other foreign broadcasts, prompting strikes and protests to break out in other cities.

By December 20 the tide had turned in Timişoara. Many rank-and-file soldiers were sickened by what they had been ordered to do and began fraternizing with the people, prompting the crowds to begin chanting: "The army is with us!" The anti-Ceauşescu plotters had apparently gained sufficient control of the military command structure to prevent further futile efforts to crush the Timişoara uprising. The first revolutionary committees were formed, and Timişoara essentially became a "free city." The main theater of resistance now shifted to Bucharest.

The Flight and Death of the Ceauşescus

Ceauşescu returned from Iran on December 20 and began to grasp the seriousness of the situation. In a speech broadcast to the nation that night he again charged that the unrest in Timişoara was an "imperialist" superpower plot designed to destroy socialism in Romania using "Fascist" Hungarian agents and hooligans. It was an unconvincing message.

The next day, December 21, Ceauşescu made the last of the many mistakes he had made during his nearly 25 years in power, and it proved to be the fatal one. He decided to greet the people, "his" people, with a rousing speech from the balcony of the Central Committee building overlooking the Palace Square. He expected applause, and why not? "Is any

"The army is with us!" A Romanian soldier on guard after the military switched to the people's side in the revolution. (AP/Wide World Photos)

dictator so entirely calculating and cynical that he can avoid falling victim to the system he creates, and himself remain undazzled by the flattery it so efficiently produces?"

This time, the crowd of thousands was not stocked with tame Ceauşescu loyalists—there were none left. Several minutes into the speech, the first shouts of "Timişoara!" and "Ceauşescu, dictator!" could be heard on the live television broadcast. Ceauşescu looked helplessly at his wife, who responded by saying, "Promise them something!" It was too late for that. The broadcast was interrupted, but before the screen went blank for good it was clear to viewers that the square had dissolved into chaos, and the entire nation could see that their vaunted emperor had no clothes.

After that epochal moment, the end came quickly. The following day, December 21, Bucharest radio announced that Defense Minister Milea had committed suicide after being exposed as a "traitor." Many observers

THE "TRIAL" OF THE CEAUŞESCUS

What follows are excerpts from a transcript of the closed military trial of Nicolae and Elena Ceauşescu, held on December 25, 1989, and broadcast the following day on Romanian television.

PROSECUTOR: Esteemed chairman of the court, today we have to pass a verdict on the defendants Nicolae Ceauşescu and Elena Ceauşescu who have committed the following offenses: Crimes against the people. They carried out acts that are incompatible with human dignity and social thinking, they acted in a despotic and criminal way, they destroyed the people whose leaders they claimed to be. Because of the crimes they committed against the people, I plead, on behalf of the victims of these two tyrants, for the death sentence for the two defendants . . .

CEAUŞESCU: I will answer any question, but only at the Grand National Assembly, before the representatives of the working class. Tell the people that I will answer all their questions. All the world should know what is going on here. I only recognize the working class and the Grand National Assembly—no one else.

PROSECUTOR: The Grand National Assembly has been dissolved.

CEAUŞESCU: This is not possible at all. No one can dissolve the National Assembly.

PROSECUTOR: We now have another leading organ. The National Salvation Front is now our supreme body.

CEAUŞESCU: No one recognizes that. That is why the people are fighting all over the country. This gang will be destroyed. They organized the putsch.

PROSECUTOR: The people are fighting against you, not against the new forum . . .

CEAUŞESCU: Nobody can change the state structures. This is not possible. Usurpers have been punished severely during the past centuries in Romania's history. Nobody has the right to abolish the Grand National Assembly.

believe he was executed by Ceauşescu after he refused to order the army to fire on the people. Whatever the case, his death helped convince wavering senior officers to throw in their lot with the revolution.

Later that day Ceauşescu made one more pathetic effort to address the crowd from his balcony, but the microphone did not work and a mob was

PROSECUTOR: Did you know about the genocide in Timişoara?

ELENA CEAUŞESCU: What genocide? By the way, I will not answer any more questions.

PROSECUTOR: Did you know about the genocide or did you, as a chemist, deal only with polymers? You, as a scientist, did you know about it?

CEAUŞESCU: Her scientific papers were published abroad!

PROSECUTOR: And who wrote the papers for you, Elena?

ELENA CEAUŞESCU: Such impudence! I am a member and the chairwoman of the Academy of Sciences. You cannot talk to me in such a way!

PROSECUTOR: You have never been able to hold a dialogue with the people . . . You held monologues and the people had to applaud, like in the rituals of tribal people. And today you are acting in the same megalomaniac way. Now we are making a last attempt. Do you want to sign this statement?

CEAUŞESCU: No, we will not sign. And I also do not recognize the counsel for the defense . . .

DEFENSE COUNSEL: Please make a note that here it has been stated that all legal regulations have been observed, that this is a legal trial. Therefore, it is a mistake for the two accused to refuse to cooperate with us. This is a legal trial and I honor them by defending them . . . I ask the court, as the plaintiff, to take note that proof has been furnished for all these points, that the two have committed the offenses mentioned. . . .

PROSECUTOR: Esteemed Mr. Chairman, I have been one of those who, as a lawyer, would have liked to oppose the death sentence, because it is inhuman. But we are not talking about people. I would not call for the death sentence, but it would be incomprehensible for the Romanian people to have to go on suffering this great misery and not to have it ended by sentencing the two Ceauşescus to death . . .

already entering the building. Ceauşescu, his wife, two top aides, and two bodyguards barely had time to climb to the roof and escape in a waiting helicopter. But their pilot betrayed them. Rather than taking them to a place of safety, he set them down on a road outside the capital. There they commandeered a car from a passing motorist but were eventually captured by soldiers and taken to an army base in the town of Tirgoviste. The base commander was ordered by the new provisional regime taking shape in Bucharest to hold them until it could send representatives to conduct a trial.

For periods over the next two days their captors kept the Ceauşescus prisoner inside an armored vehicle that kept circling around the base as protection against any rescue attempt by Securitate loyalists. On December 25, a military tribunal was hastily organized and Nicolae and Elena Ceauşescu were tried in a judicial proceeding that all observers subsequently agreed was little more than a "kangaroo court." The Ceauşescus did not recognize the authority of the tribunal and treated their prosecutors with disdain, and they in turn heaped scorn upon the accused. The "defense counsel" provided to the couple did not dispute any of the charges and insisted that the proceeding was a "legal trial." He tried in vain to convince his clients to plead insanity.

In the videotape made of the closed hearing the prosecutors' faces are not shown. However, it seemed the protagonists knew each other. "Do you know who is holding you?" a tribunal member asked at one point. "Yes," Ceauşescu replied. "Securitate." At another point, Elena said, "I was like a mother to you."

After a trial lasting several hours, the Ceauşescus were found guilty of all charges: genocide, massacre, destruction of communal property, economic subversion, attempted escape, and the hoarding of more than $1 billion in Swiss bank accounts. The sentence was death, and it was carried out virtually within minutes of the end of the trial. As the reality of their situation finally set in on the doomed couple, Elena reportedly said, "Look, they're going to shoot us like dogs. I can't believe this. Is the death penalty still in force in Romania?"

The execution was not filmed, supposedly because the eager squad of soldiers started shooting before the cameraman could get outside. The Ceauşescus were lined up against a courtyard wall and riddled with bullets. According to one account, however, the soldiers were beaten to the punch by two members of the tribunal—Virgil Magureanu and Gelu Voican Voiculescu—who killed the couple with close-range pistol shots. Both men went on to influential posts in the new government, Magureanu as head of the new intelligence service.

A videotape of the Ceauşescus' dead bodies, along with a short, edited version of the trial, was broadcast on Romanian television the next day, December 26. A longer three-hour tape of the proceedings was not released until months later. The farcical nature of the staged trial and the hasty executions struck a sour note in the minds of many Romanians and was criticized abroad. The new regime's excuse was that immediate proof of the dictator's death was necessary to convince loyalist Securitate elements who were still battling in the streets of Bucharest to give up the fight. But many people reached another conclusion, that Ceauşescu had to be killed before he could disclose secrets that the men who were maneuvering to replace him did not want revealed.

Dissident writer Paul Goma stated that by ordering the mock trial and summary executions, the new regime "stole Ceauşescu from those who suffered because of him" and "accomplished the extraordinary, the unheard and undeserved feat of turning the Ceauşescus into human beings."

The "Tele-Revolution"

The truth about the bloodshed and chaos in the city of Bucharest from December 22 to 25 remains elusive. There was fierce street fighting the likes of which had not been seen in Europe since World War II. Hundreds of people died, mostly civilians. A new, post-Ceauşescu government rose up virtually overnight, proclaiming itself the voice of the people's revolution. But the question remains: Precisely who was shooting at whom, and to what purpose?

Certain surface facts are clear. The revolution was essentially over when the Ceauşescus fled. The army, which up until that point had still been firing on demonstrators in the streets, switched its allegiance to the people—or, more specifically, to the National Salvation Front (NSF), which first proclaimed its existence in a December 22 broadcast to the nation.

Although the new ruling body included a smattering of dissident intellectuals who had taken a leading role in the uprising, the NSF consisted primarily of "former" Communist members of the Ceauşescu regime as well as ex- and current officers of the military and Securitate. Their undisputed leader was Ion Iliescu, 60, a former Ceauşescu protege who had fallen out of the dictator's good graces in the 1970s. The smoothness with which he moved into the top leadership spot reinforced speculation of the prior existence of a plot against Ceauşescu. Indeed, it was later reported that some generals switched to the side of the revolution only on the condition that "serious politicians" take power rather than "a few crazy poets and intellectuals."

However, it was just such "crazy" people—courageous would be a more accurate term—who presented the public, romantic face of the Romanian revolt that was seen by their fellow countrymen as well as by the world at large in the tumultuous days that followed. That is because Romania's was perhaps the world's first "tele-revolution." Journalists, writers, poets, and students took over Bucharest's television station and rallied the nation by broadcasting live reports of the fighting and breathless appeals to action as gunfire crackled outside the studio. As Andrei Codrescu put it, "The Revolution is Televised: Seize the Means of Projection!"—a pun on the standard Communist rhetoric about seizing the means of production.

And it was young people, mostly students, who paid the price of blood in the streets, manning barricades alongside soldiers and being shot down by mysterious snipers. Their sacrifices prompted one Romanian to reproach himself for believing that young people "had only disco, rock videos, and loud entertainment in their heads . . . What a bitter lesson in civics they taught us! What a history lesson, written in blood! How immature we so-called adults seem all of a sudden!"

These poignant images were witnessed by a worldwide audience, as one Romanian-American commentator noted:

> Watching the Romanian revolution on CNN [Cable News Network], people all over the world were struck by just how *revolutionary* the Romanian revolution was. The scenes they were seeing were reminiscent of the French and Bolshevik revolutions, living tableaux. The people atop tanks with their arms stretched in the victory sign, banners behind them . . . The tricolor armbands, the headbands . . . a beautifully photogenic but nonetheless horribly bloody revolution, summoned, it seemed, from historical skies by France itself . . .

A new, heady feeling of freedom gripped the populace in the days and weeks that followed, and common people were emboldened to speak openly to foreigners for the first time in their lives.

> It was as if they were trying to throw off a lifetime of caution in a few moments. They told us their names, their addresses, their life stories, the stories of their families, their own versions of their country's history. They even recited lists of American presidents—proud of the hitherto forbidden knowledge . . . Foreign journalists in those first few days after the revolution had become priests, privy to the unconfessed secrets of everyone.

Popular Uprising or Coup?

What was the source of the stubborn, murderous resistance against the revolution that persisted from December 22 to 25, and that waned only after the preemptive execution of the Ceauşescus? Who were the army and their civilian allies fighting against? Initially the resisters were labeled Securitate, then criminals, and finally simply terrorists. Wild, unprovable rumors circulated: The terrorists were special forces—much better armed, trained, and equipped than the regular Romanian army— from Ceauşescus's personal guard who operated outside the regular Securitate chain of command. They included a cadre of robot-like fanatics, taken as children from orphanages and raised to be brainwashed super-soldiers who would fight for their dictator with blind obedience, pumped full of drugs to make them abnormally strong. They were supported by scores of Palestinian, Libyan, and Iranian terrorists, foreign mercenaries brought into the country by helicopter to rescue Ceauşescu and wreak havoc.

The stories amounted to a mix of fact and paranoid fantasy. No solid evidence has emerged of the crazed "orphan brigade." But Ceauşescu may have had secret military agreements with Libya and Iran (whether they were ever activated is another question), and there were a few Palestinian guerrillas undergoing training in Romania who apparently became involved in the fighting. And there is no question that the terrorists were well-trained killers armed with exotic weapons—like sniper rifles with night-vision scopes—who spread panic by traveling via a secret tunnel system beneath Bucharest and popping up out of manholes to shoot unsuspecting victims.

The bloodshed was real enough. Hundreds died in Bucharest, more than had been killed in Timișoara, although interestingly most of the dead were civilians, not soldiers. (The official death toll for the entire revolution was later put at more than 1,000.) But what first raised people's suspicions was the fate of those terrorists—and there were quite a few—who were wounded, captured, or surrendered in the days after Ceaușescu's execution. They all essentially disappeared from jails and hospital beds, and none were ever brought to public trial or made available for questioning. By August 1990, the new government said it was still investigating 1,456 people, of whom 30 had been convicted and 69 others were still being tried. But all these cases involved crimes committed before December 22, 1989; that is, they were unrelated to the "terrorist" phase of the Bucharest fighting.

Iliescu himself was elusive when questioned about the identity of the "terrorists" in 1990, after he became president. "It's the most obscure problem," he said. "History will clarify these things one way or the other. It is possible that some of them will forever remain a riddle . . . I myself cannot name even those who possess all these secrets."

There were a host of other unresolved questions, some of which were obvious to anyone who examined the devastation in central Bucharest following the fighting. In Palace Square the only structure that escaped unscathed was the Central Committee building, in which the NSF leadership gathered during the crucial days and on the balcony of which they even appeared to exhort the population to resist. But nearby buildings of no obvious military significance—such as the Royal Palace, which housed the national art museum, and the university library—were virtually destroyed, at great cultural cost. Similarly, the television station survived with only a few bullet holes, while structures around it were heavily damaged or flattened. No attempt was made to blow up the TV antennae or cut power to the station.

Much of the damage was caused by indiscriminate tank fire by inexperienced soldiers. But many people wondered why the terrorists, presumably well-schooled in urban commando tactics, did not take the most obvious military steps to squelch the revolution: Attack the

NSF leadership and silence the broadcast facilities that were rallying the nation. Other questions arose in the weeks and months that followed, such as why were high-ranking army and Securitate officers implicated in the Timişoara massacre promoted to high posts in the new government.

Romanians have a national tendency to see the hidden hand of conspiracy behind most public events, but in this case they seem to be well-justified in their suspicions. The problem is that there are too many conspiracy theories to choose from, and they cannot all be correct. One major theme of the critics is that the fighting in Bucharest following Ceauşescu's fall was "an 'operetta war,' a staged affair in which only the victims were real," Nestor Ratesh wrote. "According to these critics, this mini-war was meant to legitimize the new power, to give it the aura and prestige of the savior of the revolution."

Even today, intellectuals who were themselves in the midst of the revolution are unsure what happened. "From [December] 16th to the 22nd, the fact is that the army killed the people," says writer Selian Tanase. "From the 22nd to the 25th, the army was still shooting, but we don't know who or why. I think platoons were shooting platoons." But Radu Grozea, a former academic turned television producer, has a theory: "The shooting was organized by the army as a diversion on behalf of the winners—President Iliescu—to create the idea of a civil war."

Others hypothesize that the army's motivation was not so much to bolster the new civilian leadership as to rehabilitate its own public image, which had been badly tarnished by the events in Timişoara. The staged battle against the terrorists—if that is what it was—had the additional benefit of further discrediting the Securitate, the army's long-time rival, which during Ceauşescu's regime had come to eclipse the military in power and privilege.

Certain French journalists advanced yet another theory, one remarkably similar to Ceauşescu's own: The revolution was a foreign plot devised by the Soviet Union. There is some intriguing evidence to support this theory. For example, a Soviet journalist claimed that there were nearly a dozen correspondents from TASS—the Soviet news agency that often served as cover for KGB agents—in Timişoara on December 10, five days *before* the protests began. But while Moscow may indeed have had contacts with anti-Ceauşescu conspirators dating back years, most observers agree that at best the Soviets were keenly interested observers of the Romanian revolution, not its godfather.

There is no doubt that elements in Romania's political and military elite had been plotting unsuccessfully against Ceauşescu for years, and the NSF itself had been in existence for months before the revolution. In a videotape of the NSF's chaotic "founding meeting" on December 22, Nicolae Militaru, a retired army general, can be heard saying, "Hey guys, the National Salvation Front has been in action for six months, man!"

Militaru was a key plotter and briefly served as defense minister of the new regime. In August 1990 he and Silviu Brucan went public in an interview in a Romanian newspaper with details of the long-standing anti-Ceauşescu conspiracy. (Brucan, author of the famous "Letter of Six," had served as the NSF's ideologist and spokesman before having a falling out with Iliescu.) They said the plotting against Ceauşescu had begun back in the mid-1970s, and that by the early 1980s the conspirators had settled on Iliescu as the best candidate to succeed the dictator. They said a coup had been set for 1984 but fizzled after news of it leaked.

Militaru and Brucan said that the plotters were caught by surprise by the Timişoara uprising but were able to take quick advantage of it due to their years of organizing. They gave full credit to the common people for launching the revolution, but added that "the idea that this 180-degree change [by the security forces] would have been made spontaneously is entirely mistaken . . . the dissident work within the army fully proved its political usefulness and its decisive role in preventing a bloody massacre in the whole country."

Iliescu himself in 1990 said elliptically that "we may just as well speak of several conspiracies." The question of whether the revolution was a genuine popular uprising or a coup, or an uprising cut short by a coup, continues to haunt Romanian politics to this day.

Most analysts agree that if not for the spontaneous bravery and righteous rage of the people in Timişoara and Bucharest, the revolution could not have succeeded. (At least, not at that time. Obviously Ceauşescu could not have continued in power indefinitely.) On the other hand, the people alone could not have ousted the hated dictator if the army and Securitate had stuck by him. In some ways, the coup plotters can be seen as the short-term victors, for they are the ones who seized power and prevented a more complete and radical revolution from taking place that might have tried to eradicate all aspects of the old regime.

But, despite all the political squabbling that has taken place in the years since, it is undoubtedly the Romanian people who are the long-term victors. If only for a relatively brief moment, they were masters of their own destiny, and a crushing burden was lifted from the entire national consciousness. As one Romanian journalist who witnessed the revolution firsthand put it: "Frankly, I was surprised. I did not know we Romanians had it in us."

NOTES

p. 70 "'It was like waiting for a train . . .'" Mark Frankland, *The Patriots' Revolution*, p. 316.

p. 71 "'They should have fired . . .'" Edward Behr, *Kiss the Hand You Cannot Bite*, pp. 247–248.

p. 71 "'wherever there is an attempt of [antigovernment] action, . . .'" Nestor Ratesh, *Romania: The Entangled Revolution*, p. 28.

pp. 72–73 "'Is any dictator so entirely calculating . . .'" Frankland, p. 310.

p. 74 "'What follows are excerpts . . .'" *Washington Post*, December 29, 1989.

p. 76 "'Do you know who is holding you?'" Andrei Codrescu, *The Hole in the Flag*, p. 47.

p. 76 "'Look, they are going to shoot us . . .'" Behr, p. 26.

p. 77 "'accomplished the extraordinary . . .'" Ratesh, p. 77.

p. 78 "'a few crazy poets and intellectuals.'" Ratesh, p. 52.

p. 78 "'The Revolution is Televised . . .'" Codrescu, p. 95.

p. 78 "'had only disco, rock video, and loud entertainment . . .'" Codrescu, p. 108.

p. 78 "'Watching the Romanian revolution on CNN . . .'" Codrescu, p. 105.

p. 79 "'It was as if they were trying to throw off . . .'" Codrescu, p. 103.

p. 80 "'It's the most obscure problem. . . .'" Ratesh, pp. 63–64.

p. 81 "'an "operetta war," a staged affair in which only . . .'" Ratesh, p. 62.

p. 81 "'From [December] 16th to the 22nd, . . .'" Jane Perlez, *New York Times*, December 25, 1994.

p. 81 "'The shooting was organized by the army . . .'" Perlez.

p. 81 "a Soviet journalist claimed that . . ." Codrescu, p. 171.

p. 82 "'Hey guys, the National Salvation Front . . .'" Ratesh, p. 54.

p. 82 "'the idea that this 180-degree change . . .'" Ratesh, p. 86.

p. 82 "'we may just as well speak of several conspiracies.'" Ratesh, p. 88

p. 83 "'Frankly, I was surprised. . . .'" Frankland, p. 337.

PART II
Romania Today

6
GOVERNMENT
& POLITICS

The history of Romanian politics in the decade and a half since the revolution is the story of a nation struggling to deal with the damaging
legacy of Ceauşescuism. To maintain himself in power, the dictator had
successfully atomized the entire society, preventing any alternative power
bases from arising to threaten his rule. So, unlike in other countries in
Eastern Europe, no organized dissident groups were poised to step into the
power vacuum once Ceauşescu was toppled. "There was very little in
terms of a counter-elite to create a real reform party," scholar Vladimir
Tismaneanu notes. "That explains why you have the exit of Ceauşescu
and the entrance of Iliescu."

This raises the issue of whether the rule of Ion Iliescu's National Salvation Front (NSF), despite its various name changes over the years—
and despite its being out of power from 1996 to 2000—represents what
some have called post-Communist communism, or "neocommunism."
This has been called "the paradox of the revolution: its having a clearly
anticommunist character while 'legitimating' a government that is far
from that."

However, some observers find the neocommunism label misleading
because the new leaders seem to have been motivated not so much by
ideology as by a desire to maintain power in a fragmented society unused
to freedom. In this view, "if some of communism's structures remain, it is

not because the leaders still want Marxism-Leninism but because those structures were eminently suited to concentrating political power and reproducing it."

It can also be argued that in terms of the go-slow policies they have followed, these former communist apparatchiks (officials blindly devoted to their superiors) are to some extent responding to popular pressures within Romanian society itself. For example, Western advisers and investors have clamored for Romania to move more quickly to privatize certain core sectors of its economy, particularly mining and heavy industry. But the country's various governments have resisted because such privatization would require large-scale layoffs among its core working-class supporters.

This held true even between 1996–2000 when President Emil Constantinescu and his anticommunist center-right Democratic Convention of Romania (DCR) held power. The very fact that the country's voters were able to peacefully replace Iliescu with Constantinescu, and then reelect Iliescu four years later when the DCR wasn't able to deliver on its promises (Romania's economy continued to stagnate), is an indication of how relatively normal Romania has become. The vote of the people now actually counts for something. This first step is a minimum requirement in the country's long-term dream of joining the European Union.

Certainly the situation in Romania today is light-years ahead of the darkness of the Ceauşescu era. Romanians have a new constitution, an elected, multiparty parliament, independent unions, a lively press that is free (if not entirely independent), the right to travel and associate without restriction, and the right to express political views openly.

For all the economic hardship and political strife that have characterized Romania's transition to democracy, it is perhaps those last two rights that are the revolution's most tangible benefits for ordinary citizens. As one Romanian journalist said, "I have the right to an opinion which I can express freely, and I have the right to a passport which I couldn't dream of before."

Elections and Unrest

The first two years of the new Romania was a chaotic period of rebuilding and unrest. The groundwork was gradually laid for a more democratic system, but before these new structures could establish stable roots, politics was exercised in a manner that could hardly be differentiated from street brawling.

Among its first actions in late 1989, the NSF changed the country's official name to simply Romania, dropping the title of "Socialist Republic"; declared an end to the constitutional monopoly on power by the Romanian Communist Party (RCP); canceled the destructive rural urbanization or "systemization" program; and promised early elections in 1990. Pending those elections, the country was initially ruled by a triumvirate: Iliescu as interim president, Dumitru Mazilu (a dissident former Securitate officer and diplomat) as interim vice-president, and Petre Roman (a youthful, 44-year-old engineering professor with no prior political background) as interim premier.

The new government's honeymoon was over within days. Large protests were staged in Bucharest in January 1990 demanding a purge of all Communists and the complete dismantling of the hated Securi-

tate secret police. Startled, the NSF regime said it would outlaw the Romanian Communist Party, but it then went back on its word a few days later, saying such a move would be

The honeymoon is over: In January 1990 in Bucharest, a protester against the new National Salvation Front government holds a sign equating communism and fascism. (AP/Wide World Photos)

unconstitutional. (A smaller-version RCP was revived later in the year under a new name, the Socialist Labor Party.) The NSF also reversed its initial pledge not to participate in the forthcoming elections as a political party. The broken promises touched off new demonstrations and prompted Mazilu to resign in protest against the "Stalinist methods of the new leadership."

Just as in the revolution, the new protests were led by intellectuals and students. The NSF responded by mobilizing its own partisans, including factory workers who chanted the uninspired slogan: "We work; we don't think." In late January, pro-government mobs ransacked the offices of the opposition National Peasants' Party and National Liberal Party, the two main parties of the prewar period that had been revived after the revolution.

As the unrest continued in February, the regime agreed to share power with the opposition in a Provisional National Unity Council in the run-up to the election, but the new body remained dominated by the NSF. At

Peasants and Roma (Gypsies) line up in May 1990 to vote in Romania's first mostly free election in more than 50 years. (AP/Wide World Photos)

the request of the opposition, the voting was delayed for a month to allow more time for them to organize. It hardly helped: On May 20, in Romania's first free election in more than 50 years, the NSF won 65 percent of the seats in the new parliament, and Iliescu was elected president with 85 percent of the vote. More than 14 million of the country's 16 million eligible voters went to the polls.

International observers backed opposition claims of widespread voting irregularities, and there is no question that NSF supporters used intimidation, harassment, and other illegal tactics in the period leading up to the election and during the voting itself. But even allowing for vote-rigging and fraud, it was clear that the vast majority of Romanians—mostly conservative peasants and workers who did not share the views of the intellectual class—chose the continuity represented by the NSF, preferring the known to the unknown.

The election did little to bring political peace. Earlier in April, students had organized a permanent occupation of Bucharest's University Square, where tens of thousands of people gathered in what they declared a "Communist-free zone" to protest the government. After the election the crowds dwindled, but the encampment continued until mid-June, when police moved in and brutally attacked the protesters. That provoked an angry mob to march on government buildings and storm the television station.

With the police and army showing no willingness to confront the rioters, President Iliescu appealed to the working class to "save the democracy" from a "Fascist rebellion." On June 14, the government brought more than 10,000 coal miners from the Jiu Valley by train and truck into central Bucharest, where they were greeted by the president and then set loose to "restore order." Over the next two days the miners, armed with clubs and crowbars, savagely attacked and beat hundreds of students, Gypsies, and other perceived opponents and ransacked the offices of political opposition parties. The official death toll was six, with many serious injuries, while more than 1,000 people were detained. At a mass farewell rally June 15, Iliescu personally thanked the miners for "doing very good work," adding, "If I need you again, I will call you."

The government-sanctioned violence drew strong international condemnation, and in protest the U.S. ambassador to Romania boycotted Iliescu's official inauguration as president in late June. The heavy-handed repression reinforced the view that Romania remained the least reformed of Eastern Europe's formerly Communist states and made it more difficult to attract foreign aid and trade.

The events of June 1990 in some ways remain as mysterious as those of December 1989. Opposition figures charged that the unrest had been orchestrated by "rogue" Securitate agents who first acted as provocateurs in the antigovernment riots and then directed some of the worst excesses of the miners. Analysts agree that the violence was a sign that the NSF was far from monolithic, and that opposing factions both inside and outside the government—including elements of both the army and the Securitate—were engaged in a shadowy, behind-the-scenes struggle for power.

The government of Premier Roman continued to be beset with large-scale protests against the country's deteriorating economy. The regime instituted some economic reforms, including limited privatization of state enterprises and the lifting of price controls. Reacting to the price increases, a new opposition movement, the Civic Alliance, staged a protest of 100,000 people in Bucharest in November 1990, and workers in Timişoara called a general strike the following month.

The popular protests did not let up in 1991. In September the Jiu Valley miners returned to Bucharest, but this time they came to confront the government. They demanded wage increases, a price freeze, and the resignation of both Iliescu and Roman. Joined by students and other antigovernment protesters (the same people the miners had beaten the previous year), the miners stormed the parliament and other government buildings, attacked the television station, and besieged the presidential palace. Violent clashes with security forces left at least four people dead.

The crisis forced Roman and his cabinet to resign. Iliescu appointed Theodor Stolojan, a former finance minister, as the new premier. Meanwhile, the conspiracy mill continued to churn. It was rumored that Iliescu had plotted with the miners to oust Roman (the president had begun to differ with his premier over the pace of economic reform). Others blamed the latest unrest, again, on the Securitate, or else on right-wingers seeking to topple the NSF.

The year ended on a more positive note when the parliament approved a new constitution in November and it was endorsed by 77 percent of voters in a national referendum in December. The new charter defined Romania as a multiparty presidential republic. It vested strong powers in the presidency, guaranteed human rights and ethnic diversity, and banned capital punishment and torture. The constitution also backed a free-market economy and the right to own private property, although it forbade foreigners from owning Romanian land.

There were further changes in the country's political landscape in 1992, but this time the changes were free of serious violence. In February and March the first post-Communist elections were held at the local level for seats on city and town councils. The voting confirmed a precipitous decline in the NSF's popularity: Its candidates won only about 33 percent of the races, a halving of its support from the 1990 national elections. The Democratic Convention of Romania (DCR), a newly formed alliance of 18 opposition parties from the political center-right, won nearly 25 percent of the seats. The DCR's strength was centered in major cities like Bucharest, Braşov, Sibiu, Arad, and Timişoara, while the NSF ran stronger in rural areas.

The NSF Splits

The electoral setback led to a split in the NSF, as the feud between Roman and Iliescu erupted into the open. Following his forced resignation the previous fall, Roman had begun attacking the president, his former mentor, as a "neocommunist" opposed to reform. Iliescu responded by calling Roman a "political playboy" and a "political soldier of fortune" who had betrayed the NSF's social democratic principles. In March 1992 there was a formal separation: Roman became president of the now centrist NSF while Iliescu and his followers split off to form the more leftist Democratic National Salvation Front (DNSF)—which, since Iliescu was president, automatically became the ruling party.

Romania held its second post-revolution general election in September 1992. The DNSF won 28 percent of the seats in parliament, the DCR alliance about 20 percent and the NSF 10 percent, with the remaining seats split among five smaller parties. In the first round of the presidential voting, no candidate won more than 50 percent, necessitating a runoff between the two top finishers, Iliescu and Emil Constantinescu, a political novice endorsed by the DCR. In the second round of voting in October, Iliescu won with about 61 percent of the vote.

In the campaign Iliescu and the DNSF had taken advantage of the anxieties felt by farmers and workers in the transition to a free-market economy, labeling Constantinescu and the DCR as supporters of mass unemployment and "wild capitalism." The DNSF also had the support of the *nomenklatura*, the former Communist bureaucrats and managers who still controlled much of the country's economy. Iliescu's critics charged that the DNSF was a haven for die-hard ex-Communists.

In November, Iliescu appointed, and the new parliament confirmed, Nicolae Vacaroiu as premier, replacing, Stolojan, who had been in office only a year. Vacaroiu—an economist who opposed radical reform and called for a slower transition to capitalism—then assembled a cabinet that included equal numbers of DNSF members and independents.

In 1993, the ruling DNSF merged with three smaller left-wing parties to form the Party of Social Democracy in Romania (PSDR). Adrian Nastase was elected the party's executive chairman, while Iliescu remained the party's "moral guide," "patriarch," and "guru." (Technically, the new Romanian constitution did not allow the country's president to be formally affiliated with any political party.) Meanwhile, Petre Roman's opposition NSF joined with the tiny Democratic Party and rechristened itself the Democratic Party-National Salvation Front (DP-NSF).

Vacaroiu's minority PSDR government continued to defy predictions of its imminent demise. Despite corruption scandals and numerous attempts by the opposition to bring down the government through parliamentary motions of no-confidence, it somehow clung to power, owing in part to disunity among the opposition. By July 1994, it had survived five no-confidence votes, even though opinion polls showed that 74 percent of the public did not think it was doing a good job.

The Rise of Extremism

One distinctly negative political development during this period was the rise in power and influence of several extremist ultranationalist parties. These include the Transylvania-based Party of Romanian National Unity, led by Gheorghe Funar, the mayor of Cluj; the Greater Romania Party, led by Corneliu Vadim Tudor; and the Socialist Labor Party (the former Communist Party). All three won parliamentary seats in the 1992 elections and

A burnt-out Securitate building in Sibiu after the revolution. People are searching the rubble for any secret files that may have survived. (AP/Wide World Photos)

Tudor went on to win significant support in the 2000 presidential election. They share similar traits: They are strongly anti-Semitic and anti-Hungarian, they blame foreigners (and their domestic "agents") for all of Romania's problems, and they advocate a policy of "radical continuity" with the national communism of the former Ceaușescu dictatorship.

These parties represent a curious "red-brown" coalition (red being the symbolic color of communism and brown the color of fascism). Along with their nostalgia for Ceaușescuism, the extremist parties have also been seeking to rehabilitate the reputation of Marshal Ion Antonescu, Romania's Fascist dictator during World War II. A statue honoring Antonescu was erected in the town of Slobozia in October 1993, and a governmental official attended the dedication ceremony, prompting a protest by the United States. As Andrei Codrescu said, "It is as if a statue of, let's say, the founder of the Ku Klux Klan were erected in Washington in a ceremony attended by Administration officials."

In defending Antonescu, extremist leader Tudor told a Jewish historian: "If Antonescu had been a Hitler, you may rest assured that today we would not be watching you and [Chief Rabbi] Moses Rosen on the television screen in cultural programs but rather as ads for Palmolive, Camay . . .

FACTS ON ILIESCU

Romania's President Ion Iliescu was born on March 3, 1930, son of one of the few members of the prewar Romanian Communist Party. He became a leader of the Communist Youth Union as a teenager and was sent to Moscow in 1950 for training as a hydroelectric engineer. But he chose politics over a technical career, and with his impeccable Communist credentials he rose rapidly up the party ladder. By age 35 he was a member of the Central Committee and in 1967 he became minister for youth affairs. He was named Central Committee secretary in charge of ideology in 1971, but that same year he had a falling out with Ceau-şescu after accompanying him on his visit to China and North Korea.

Iliescu says the dictator "was literally fascinated by Korea . . . [It] was the perfect model of an absolute totalitarianism. On our return, he drew up a kind of platform for a cultural revolution Romanian style. That was the break."

For his disagreement Iliescu was demoted to the provinces, but he gradually worked his way back to the party's Political Executive Committee later in the 1970s. In 1984 Ceauşescu stripped him of all his party and government positions, perhaps because of suspicions that he was somehow involved in a purported coup plot that fizzled that year.

"I was somehow known as one who was not in Ceauşescu's favor, because I used to express my opinions in a very direct way." He ended up as director of the Bucharest State Technical Publishing House, a post he still held at the time of the 1989 revolution.

President Ion Iliescu. (AP/Wide World Photos)

and other brands of soap." (This was a sickening reference to the Nazi practice of using the remains of death camp victims to make soap.)

Such vicious rhetoric has become common in the nationalist press, and the extremist parties have been given extensive coverage on state-run television. President Iliescu condemned the resurgence of anti-Semitism, but the ruling Party of Social Democracy in Romania has come to depend on the parliamentary support of these radical parties to remain in power. At first that cooperation was informal, but in August 1994 the Party of Romanian National Unity, or PRNU, officially joined the government (among the cabinet posts it controlled was the justice ministry). Then, after months of haggling, in January 1995 the PSDR signed a protocol with the three main radical parties, formally cementing its alliance with the extremists in an arrangement popularly known as the "red quadrangle."

The party's Chairman Nastase admitted the new coalition was a "sensitive" issue that might harm Romania's image abroad, but he claimed that the extremists would now be forced to behave more responsibly. As if to prove that was wishful thinking, the PRNU promptly embarrassed the government by launching an anti-Semitic attack on Alfred Moses, the new U.S. ambassador to Bucharest.

Despite such virulent extremism, the PRNU remained in the ruling coalition for more than two years, until September 1996, when the PSDR ousted its members from the cabinet. The final straw came after party leader Georghe Funar called a pending treaty with Hungary "an act of national treason" and called for the impeachment of Iliescu. (Details of the treaty will be covered in subsequent chapters.)

Many Romanians remained suspicious of the continuing power of those associated with the worst excesses of the Securitate under the Ceauşescu regime. These feelings were not alleviated by the special military tribunals held in 1990 and 1991 in which a number of Ceauşescu loyalists, including high-ranking Securitate officers, were sentenced to long prison terms for ordering the shootings in Timişoara and Bucharest. Most of those sentences were later quietly reduced or even commuted under a general amnesty. Those let off lightly included Nicu Ceauşescu, the dictator's son, who was given a 20-year sentence in September 1990 but freed in November 1992 on grounds of ill health. (He died of cirrhosis of the liver in 1996 at the age of 45.)

The Opposition Gets Its Chance

In June 1996, nationwide elections were again held for mayors and local officials, and the opposition DCR made further gains at the expense of the ruling PSDR. That was a harbinger of a growing shift in Romanian politics that reached its climax just five months later.

On November 3, Romanians voted in national elections for president and parliament, and the opposition triumphed. The center-right DCR and centrist Social Democratic Union (SDU)—the new name for Petre Roman's DP-NSF—together won 213 seats in the 343-member Chamber of Deputies and 94 seats in the 143-member Senate. The two parties quickly signed an agreement to govern together as a coalition, along with the smaller Hungarian Democratic Union of Romania. The presidential voting was much tighter: Iliescu led with 32 percent, the DCR's Constantinescu received 29 percent, and Roman trailed with nearly 21 percent. Thirteen other minor candidates also ran.

Since no candidate received a majority, a runoff election between the two top finishers was held on November 17, 1996. It was a repeat of their 1992 matchup, but this time Constantinescu beat Iliescu by a solid margin of 54 to 46 percent. It seemed Romanians had decided to give the other side a chance, and it was a tribute to the country's fledgling democracy that Iliescu and the PSDR accepted the verdict of the people. The transfer of power occurred peacefully.

Emil Constantinescu was born in Moldova in 1939. He studied geology and law and joined the Communist Party, though he never held an official party post. During the revolution, he took part in demonstrations against Ceauşescu, and later joined the opposition Civic Alliance. In April 1990, as rector of Bucharest University, he supported students protesting against Iliescu.

As in 1992, in 1996 Constantinescu ran as a reformer, vowing to fight corruption and finally modernize the decrepit economy. Because of his more conservative background, Romanians viewed Constantinescu as someone who could succeed where Iliescu had failed in attracting Western investment. They believed he could pave the way for the country's entry into NATO and, ultimately, the European Union.

As his first premier, Constantinescu named the DCR's Victor Ciorbea, who in June had been elected mayor of Bucharest, beating former tennis star and PSDR candidate Ilie Nastase. It was an auspicious beginning, but it gradually became apparent to Romania's downtrodden population that the more things changed, the more they seemed to stay the same, if not actually to get worse.

It turned out the anticommunists were no better at running the economy than the former communists, and the country slid into a punishing three-year recession that saw its already low standard of living sink still lower. Some reforms were carried out, but core money-losing industrial sectors remained stubbornly resistant to privatization, and foreign investors were put off by the government's continued bureaucratic inertia and corruption. While Constantinescu and Ciorbea had reputations for honesty, it appears there were other officials who followed in the footsteps of their PSDR predecessors, demanding bribes and using insider privatization schemes to enrich themselves at the public's expense.

However, more than corruption, it was the virtually constant political squabbling and infighting within the various parties of the ruling coalition—many of them new to power—that doomed the government to paralysis. Ciorbea lasted some 16 months, until March 30, 1998, when he resigned under heavy pressure from junior parties in the coalition. He was replaced by Radu Vasile, who managed to hang on until December 1999, when Constantinescu replaced him with Mugur Isarescu after 10 members of the cabinet resigned in protest over Vasile's leadership. The key portfolio of finance minister became a similar revolving door, with three different men—Mircea Ciumara, Daniel Daianu, and Decebal Train Remes—holding the post during the government's four-year run. In each case, the reason given for the dismissals was failure to reform the economy.

The difficulty of effecting such reforms was made clear in January 1999, when Romania experienced an outbreak of mob violence of the sort it hadn't seen in nearly eight years. Once again it involved coal miners from the Jiu Valley, who commenced a march on Bucharest to protest two proposed mine closings and to demand higher wages. Under the leadership of Miron Cozma, the miners broke through barricades and injured an estimated 200 policemen. As one reporter noted:

> The miners outwitted police officers by using such medieval tactics as rolling down huge stones from the surrounding hills, a possibility inexplicably ignored by those responsible for police deployment. In a

country where conspiracy theories are one of the media's favorite occupations, this has led to speculation that the forces of law and order were "betrayed from within." On this occasion, there seems to have been at least some truth to the speculation. Deputy Interior Minister Viorel Oancea confirmed that the miners appeared to have inside information.

Whatever their links to shadowy forces within the government, in the end the miners stopped only when officials negotiated a "mysterious agreement" to keep the two money-losing mines open and increase wages. But the Vasile government struck back the following month by arresting Cozma—dubbed "public enemy number one"—and sentencing him to 18 years in prison for his role in leading the violent Bucharest riots that toppled the Petre Roman government in 1991. One miner was killed and 20 police injured in protests accompanying the arrest, which officials said was critical to preserving judicial authority and overcoming opposition to market reforms.

The Return of Iliescu

By the end of its four-year term, the DCR-led government was so unpopular that Constantinescu chose not to stand for reelection, and instead endorsed Premier Mugur Isarescu to run in his place in the November 2000 elections. Showing how far the center-right coalition's fortunes had fallen, he managed to garner only nine percent of the vote. Even more surprising was the 28 percent won by the infamous far-right extremist Corneliu Vadim Tudor, who finished second behind former President Iliescu of the PSDR and his 37 percent of the vote. (Nine other candidates also ran.)

The PSDR (which shortened its name to the Party of Social Democracy or PSD) managed to win a plurality but not an outright majority in parliament. However, Tudor's ultranationalist Greater Romania Party won 25 percent of the seats, making it the largest opposition party. It was quite a turnaround: in 1996, Tudor and the GRP had received less than four percent of the vote. But to keep the extremists out of the government—which would have severely hurt Romania's image in Europe—the

PSD decided to form a minority government with the tacit parliamentary support of the centrist parties.

Once again, the presidential election went to a runoff, and in the two weeks leading up to the vote, both candidates ran against their records. Iliescu promised this time he really would reform the economy, even at the expense of mass layoffs, while Tudor vowed not to harm ethnic minorities (Hungarians, Gypsies, and Jews) and expressed regret for his previous anti-Semitic diatribes.

Still, Tudor could only tame himself so much. In a televised speech, he proclaimed: "The scum of the revolution has grown thicker in these 11 years, and Romania has been transformed into a mafia state." Iliescu responded that Tudor's speech was "full of demagoguery, incoherent thinking, and megalomania." Many in the independent press took a "pox-on-both-your-houses" approach, with one newspaper editorializing about having to "choose between AIDS and cancer."

On December 10, with only 57 percent of the electorate participating, Iliescu beat Tudor by a margin of 67 to 33 percent. Despite that resounding victory for the establishment, many Romanians and foreign observers expressed dismay that fully one-third of the voters had cast their ballots for what could only be called a neofascist candidate.

Iliescu named Adrian Nastase premier, and he quickly began forming a government to try to turn around a country that seemed to have gone terribly off-course. Tudor's voters were "a mix of the extreme left and extreme right, and a result of the deep frustration from an important part of the population," Nastase acknowledged in a 2001 interview. Mircea Geoana, the new foreign minister, agreed that "terrible social conditions and the last election were a cold shower for us all, a real wake-up call. . . . Now we're scared—we know that this time we really have to bite the bullet."

The Exiled King

No discussion of Romanian politics would be complete without mention of King Michael, who was forced to abdicate and flee into exile in Switzerland after the 1947 Communist takeover. In 1990, the king tried to visit Romania but was stopped at the airport by the new government.

When he was finally permitted to visit in April 1992, he received a tumultuous welcome from thousands of Romanians in Bucharest.

Perhaps because of that enthusiastic reception, the next time he tried to visit—in October 1994—the king was again denied entry at the airport. President Iliescu claimed that Michael, 74, represented a threat to "Romania's public constitutional order." But most Romanian analysts discounted any such threat, saying the basis of the king's popularity was purely nostalgic and emotional, not political.

Michael even gave what amounted to an endorsement of Iliescu shortly before the 2000 presidential runoff vote, writing in a letter to the Associated Press: "If you give your vote to politicians who encourage ethnic and racial hate, who speak the language of violence, Romania will be left out of Europe for decades."

NOTES

p. 87 "'There was very little in terms of . . .'" Jane Perlez, *New York Times*, December 25, 1994.

p. 87 "'the paradox of the revolution: . . .'" Ivo Banac, ed., *Eastern Europe in Revolution*, p. 125.

pp. 87–88 "'if some of communism's structures remain . . .'" Banac, p. 130.

p. 88 "'I have the right to an opinion . . .'" Perlez.

p. 90 "'We work; we don't think.'" Nestor Ratesh, *Romania: The Entangled Revolution*, p. 130.

p. 91 "'doing very good work, . . .'" *Facts On File World News Digest*, June 22, 1990, p. 467A2.

p. 93 "'neocommunist . . . political playboy . . . political soldier . . .'" Michael Shafir and Dan Ionescu, *RFE/RL*, January 1, 1993.

p. 94 "'wild capitalism'" Shafir and Ionescu.

p. 94 "'moral guide . . . patriarch . . . guru'" *RFE/RL*, August 27, 1993.

p. 95 " 'It is as if a statue of . . .' " Andrei Codrescu, *New York Times*, December 7, 1993.

pp. 95, 97 "'If Antonescu had been a Hitler . . .'" Michael Shafir, *RFE/RL*, April 22, 1994.

p. 96 "'was literally fascinated by Korea . . .'" Michael Shafir, *Transition*, April 14, 1995.

p. 96 "'I was somehow known as one who . . .'" Ratesh, p. 52.

p. 97 "'red quadrangle'" Dan Ionescu, *RFE/RL*, July 29, 1994.

pp. 99–100 "'The miners outwitted police officers . . .' " Michael Shafir. "Romania: Government Comes to Mysterious Agreement With Miners," *RFE/RL*.

Available on-line. URL:http://www.rferl.org/nca/features/1999/01/F.RU. 990127134446.html. Posted on January 27, 1999.

p. 101 "'The scum of the revolution . . .'" Donald G. McNeil Jr., *New York Times,* December 10, 2000.

p. 101 "'a mix of the extreme left and extreme right . . .'" Steven Erlanger, *New York Times,* February 11, 2001.

p. 102 "'If you give your vote to . . .'" McNeil.

7

THE PEOPLE

As with many countries, Romania's sense of national identity is deeply influenced by issues of ethnicity, language, and culture. Although ethnic Romanians (those who speak Romanian as their first language and identify with Romanian culture) make up the vast majority of the population, they often define themselves as much by who they are *not*—i.e., Hungarians, Jews, etc.—as by who they *are*.

The collapse of communism has let the nationalist genie out of the bottle all over Eastern Europe. Ethnic differences that had been suppressed by strict government control of all aspects of life have once again taken center stage. Ethnic groups tend to have long historical memories and to nurse grudges against other groups that can date back centuries. Communist rule merely kept these problems hidden below the surface, where they continued to fester like an untreated wound. As one Hungarian journalist considering the Transylvania question has said, "In East Europe we all feel guilty, and we all point the finger at someone else."

In this respect, the problems Romania has faced since the revolution are no worse than many of those that have arisen in other Eastern European states. Indeed, after observing the ethnic and religious civil wars that ripped apart neighboring Yugoslavia, it is amazing that Romania's group relations have remained as peaceful as they have, considering the country's complicated history.

Before going any further into Romania's ethnic situation, it will be useful to look at some basic statistics concerning the country's population

Scenes of rural life in Romania sometimes seem to be from an earlier time. This old woman is carrying her load in the village of Uzunu. (AP/Wide World Photos)

and demographics. As of July 2002, Romania had an estimated population of 22,317,730, a slight decrease from a decade earlier. Of that total, 19,952,922 (89.4 percent) are Romanians and 365,602 (10.6 percent) are members of ethnic minorities. The latter break down as follows: 7.1 percent Hungarians (Magyars and Szeklers), 1.8 percent Gypsies or Roma, (although that may be a significant undercount), 0.5 percent Germans (Saxons and Swabians), 0.3 percent Ukrainians, and 0.04 percent Jews. The remainder consists of Serbians, Croats, Russians, Czechs, Slovaks, Slovenes, Bulgarians, Turks, and Tartars. An estimated 8 million Romanians live outside the national boundaries, most of them in Moldova, Ukraine, Hungary, Albania, Bulgaria, and Yugoslavia.

According to the latest figures, the country's religious makeup consists of approximately 70 percent Romanian Orthodox, 6 percent Roman Catholic (mostly Hungarians and Germans), 3 percent Uniate Catholic, 6 percent Protestant, and 18 percent unaffiliated. (Many of the latter category are sometimes classified as being nominally Romanian Orthodox.)

While the constitution provides for religious freedom, the U.S. State Department has noted that several minority denominations continue to allege that low-level government officials and Romanian Orthodox clergy have impeded their efforts to proselytize. The Romanian press has reported instances when adherents of minority religions were prevented from practicing their faith and did not receive protection from local law enforcement authorities.

The country's average population density is 95.7 inhabitants per square mile and is heaviest in central and southwestern Walachia and central and northwestern Transylvania. The population concentrated in urban areas amounts to 54.3 percent, a significantly lower percentage than elsewhere in Europe. This distribution of the population is illustrated by the fact that while Bucharest has more than 2 million inhabitants, the next seven largest cities—Constanța, Iași, Timișoara, Cluj-Napoca, Galati, Brașov, and Craiova—have populations of 350,000 or less.

Most of the areas of the Old Kingdom (Walachia and Moldavia) continue to be ethnically homogeneous, with many districts essentially 100 percent inhabited by Romanians. Among the exceptions are northern Moldavia and Bukovina, which until World War II had significant numbers of Jews; Dobruja, where there is a large percentage of Bulgarians, Russians, Tartars, and Turks; and Bucharest, which has large Hungarian and Gypsy communities.

But clearly the most ethnically heterogeneous regions of Romania are Transylvania and the Banat (the two areas are often lumped together). This area is home to most of Romania's Hungarian- and German-speaking population. More than 20 percent of Transylvania's people are Hungarian.

The Hungarian Question

The long history behind the dispute between Romanians and Hungarians in Transylvania has been covered in detail in earlier chapters. What follows is an account of how that struggle has manifested itself in the years since the 1989 revolution.

Following Ceaușescu's overthrow, Hungarian activists began demanding greater use of the Hungarian language in education and on street signs. Romanian ultranationalists responded by organizing a quasi-Fascist organization, *Vatra Romaneasca* (Romanian Cradle, or Hearth), and its political arm, the Party of Romanian National Unity (PRNU). When Hungarians staged a demonstration in the town of Tirgu Mures in March 1990 they were violently attacked by a mob of Romanian extremists, sparking two days of riots in which five people were killed (three Romanians and two Hungarians) and troops were called out to restore order.

In a bid for the support of the ultranationalists, the National Salvation Front government placed all the blame for the incident on the Hungarians, whom President Iliescu labeled "hooligans." His foreign minister claimed, "It is not the NSF that has alienated the Hungarian minority. The Hungarian minority has decided to alienate itself from the NSF." In subsequent general elections, the Hungarian Democratic Union of Romania (HDUR) became a significant opposition force in the national parliament.

Tensions worsened after a leading Romanian extremist, Gheorghe Funar, was elected mayor of the city of Cluj in February 1992. (He later became leader of the Party of Romanian National Unity.) He immediately began a campaign to expunge the Hungarian language from public use, beginning with the removal of the city's bilingual street signs. Later in the year, ethnic Hungarian prefects in two Transylvanian districts were replaced by Romanians, and the only Hungarian state secretary in the national government lost his post. In 1993 the government sought to ease tensions by signing an agreement on minority rights that supposedly provided for the training of Hungarian-speaking schoolteachers and guaranteed bilingual street signs in areas with a Hungarian population of at least 30 percent.

However, attempts to "Romanize" the Hungarian minority continued to gain ground throughout the country in 1994, worsening relations between Romania and Hungary. Extremist parties helped push a bill through the lower house of parliament that would ban church-sponsored Hungarian language schools. Laszlo Tokes, the Hungarian pastor who helped spark the Timişoara uprising in December 1989, said the new law was "totally discriminatory, worse than in the times of Ceauşescu."

Meanwhile, Funar sponsored an archaeological dig in Cluj's main square that, although ostensibly aimed at finding the ruins of an ancient

Roman forum, would coincidentally also require the removal of a statue of Hungary's 15th-century King Mathias. Thousands of Hungarians rallied to block the start of the excavation. "That statue embodies our community consciousness and our history," Tokes said. "It's the symbol of our struggle for rights in the face of 75 years of humiliation."

On the other side, Cluj deputy prefect and Party of Romanian National Unity member Liviu Medrea declared: "In Romania, the time has passed when those belonging to an ethnic minority group can dictate to us . . . We are sure that truth and right are on our side."

Despite the continued hostility of such extremist groups, the situation improved markedly after Romania and Hungary signed a treaty in 1996 demarcating their common border and guaranteeing the rights of ethnic minorities. It further helped that year when the HDUR went from being an opposition party to joining the coalition government of President Emil Constantinescu, which was eager to improve its human rights record to help gain entry into the European Union.

The HDUR is divided between a more militant camp that advocates political autonomy led by Laszlo Tokes and a larger and more moderate faction that stresses cultural and educational rights led by Marko Bela. A government decree that went into effect in 1999 permitted Hungarian minority students in state-funded primary and secondary schools to be taught in their own language, with the exception of secondary school courses on Romania's history and geography.

Exodus

Although most of Romania's ethnic Hungarians showed every sign of staying put, many other Romanians have continued to vote with their feet and flee the country as both political and economic refugees. In the latter years of Ceauşescu's rule, Romania had become "a foremost supplier of refugees to other countries." The flood of emigrants grew even larger after the revolution, with thousands swarming into Western Europe, particularly Germany. By late 1993, one-quarter of all those seeking asylum in Germany were from Romania (many of them Gypsies).

One survey estimated that 250,000 Romanian citizens had sought asylum abroad between 1990 and 1993. Another 1.5 million Romanians

—most of them young and well-educated—were said to be considering emigration.

Not all of the Romanian exodus was haphazard or unplanned. During the 1980s, the West German government had paid the Ceauşescu regime large sums to allow tens of thousands of ethnic Germans to return to their motherland. The process continued after the revolution, and in 1990 an estimated 120,000 members of Romania's German-speaking community (known as Saxons and Swabians) immigrated to Germany.

The Jewish exodus was even more complete. The Israeli government had also paid Ceauşescu to allow the mass immigration of Romania's Jews to Israel. Of the 400,000 Jews who survived the Romanian Holocaust, all but 20,000 had left by 1989. That number continued to dwindle still further as anti-Semitism mounted in Romania after the revolution. By the

THE PLIGHT OF THE ROMA

Two-thirds of Europe's 8 million Gypsies live in Central and Eastern Europe. Romania has the largest concentration of them all. The 1992 census put Romania's total at around 400,000, but many experts consider that a serious underestimate, whether deliberate or otherwise. Some put the real number at around 1.5 million. In their own language Gypsies prefer to call themselves Roma (considering "Gypsy" to be an insult), although that has nothing to do with Romania; they are descendants of a people who first reached Europe in the 11th century after a long migration from India. Traditionally they are a nomadic people who live in rural encampments and move from place to place, supporting themselves with temporary menial work and sometimes with illegal activities, although many have settled in cities and hold regular jobs.

Just as the fall of communism has unleashed latent currents of anti-Semitism across Eastern Europe, so has it sharpened widespread public hostility toward the Roma. They "are generally persecuted by the police, humiliated by the local authorities and made to live on the margin," one Romanian human rights activist says. "There is a large campaign to present Gypsies all the time as criminals, in the press and television, and this is perpetuated by teachers. This is a tragedy of our schools."

time of the January 1992 census, the number of Jews remaining in the country was put at only 8,955.

Rhetorical attacks on Jews in Romania—and in Eastern Europe generally—often take the form of blaming the Jews for communism. While Jews had played a disproportionate role in the early days of the Romanian Communist Party, virtually all of them were later purged from power, a process finished by Ceaușescu in the 1970s. "Most of these fanatical Jewish communists ended up in Israel after they were thrown out of their jobs," according to Romania's Chief Rabbi Moses Rosen. "Now they're all big Zionists."

Perhaps more than any people in Eastern Europe, Romanians have had difficulty coming to terms their country's role in the extermination of the Jews during the Holocaust. (See chapter 3.) In July 2002,

---

In 1991 there were organized attacks on Roma communities throughout Romania, prompting thousands to flee the country, mostly to Germany. (In September 1992 the German government sent 43,000 Romanian refugees, more than half of them Roma, back to Romania after agreeing to pay millions of dollars for their resettlement.) The attacks continued over the next two years, and after almost every incident the authorities arrested only Roma, blaming them for provoking the clashes.

One of the worst occurred in the Transylvanian village of Hadreni in September 1993 after a large gang attacked four young Roma men. One of the Romanian attackers was stabbed to death, after which hundreds of villagers set fire to the house in which the Roma had taken refuge and then killed three of them as they tried to escape the flames. The mob then burned and destroyed more than a dozen Roma homes. No arrests were made. The deputy mayor, asked if the Roma could ever forget what had happened, replied: "We hope they will. They know it was their fault."

Such large-scale attacks waned in the years that followed, and the Roma community has gradually become more politically assertive. In May 2001, several Roma groups established the Roma Federation, which planned to monitor the implementation of the Strategy for the Improvement of the Roma Situation that the government had adopted the previous month.

Romanian-born U.S. author and human rights advocate Elie Wiesel, winner of the 1986 Nobel Peace Prize, inaugurated a Jewish museum in Sighet, Transylvania, in the house that had been his boyhood home and from which he and his family had been deported in 1944 to the Auschwitz concentration camp in Poland. Accompanying Wiesel, 73, on his visit was President Ion Iliescu, who Wiesel credited with the idea for the museum.

In a previous visit to the country in 1991, Wiesel had been heckled while delivering a speech deploring the Romanian parliament's decision to honor the memory of World War II fascist leader Marshal Ion Antonescu. The new museum did not directly address Antonescu's wartime record of atrocities against Jews, but focused instead on the fate of the Jewish community in the Nazi- and Hungarian-occupied region around Sighet.

In response to warnings that Romania's chances to join NATO could be hurt by statues of Antonescu and streets named after him, Iliescu's government banned public displays of his image, though the law was

Nobel laureate Elie Wiesel, center, observes a traditional Romanian cross in the "merry cemetery" in Sapanta with President Ion Iliescu in July 2002. Wiesel was on a visit to inaugurate a Jewish museum in Sighet. (AP/Wide World Photos)

unpopular and not rigorously enforced. "You can attack the cult of Antonescu, but you can't rewrite history," said Premier Adrian Nastase. To which Wiesel responded: "Do not turn your back on the past. Integrate it into your life and you will flourish. Forget it and you are doomed."

The Hidden Minority

The most invisible of all minorities in Romania are gays and lesbians. In fact, despite the international controversy it causes, homosexuality is still illegal. The old criminal code inherited from the communist era stated that "sexual relations between persons of the same sex are punishable by imprisonment of one to five years."

In the 1990s, Romania came under increasing pressure from the Council of Europe and Amnesty International to undo the repressive legislation, and gay and lesbian groups organized international protests and called for a worldwide boycott of Romanian wine. In response, after intense debate in 1996, parliament amended the law in a way that officials described as a liberalization. In fact, the new version actually expanded the law to provide for imprisonment for homosexual acts "committed in public, or if causing a public scandal," as well as "propaganda or association or any other acts of proselytism."

Human-rights activists say the law will continue to be a sticking point with other European countries as Romania lobbies to join the EU in the years ahead.

NOTES
p. 105 "'In East Europe we all feel guilty, . . .'" Mark Frankland, *The Patriots' Revolution*, p. 339.
p. 108 "'It is not the NSF that has alienated the . . .'" Gale Stokes, *The Walls Came Tumbling Down*, p. 174.
p. 108 "'totally discriminatory, worse than . . .'" David B. Ottaway, *Washington Post*, July 5, 1994.
p. 109 "'That statue embodies our community consciousness . . .'" Ottaway.
p. 109 "'In Romania, the time has passed . . .'" Ottaway.
p. 109 "'a foremost supplier of refugees . . .'" Michael Shafir, *RFE/RL*, June 24, 1994.
p. 110 "'are generally persecuted by the police . . .'" Henry Kamm, *New York Times*, November 17, 1993.

p. 111 "'Now they're all big Zionists.'" Charles Hoffman, *Gray Dawn*, p. 131.

p. 111 "'We hope they will. They know it was their fault.'" Henry Kamm, *New York Times*, October 27, 1993.

p. 113 "'You can attack the cult of Antonescu . . .'" Daniel Simpson, *New York Times*, July 31, 2002.

8
THE ECONOMY

Romanians could forgive their government a multitude of political sins as long as it delivered on its basic promises of ensuring economic stability and growth. So far, the record remains extremely mixed, no matter which side—the Left or the Right—has been in power. It's been the old "one-two"—one step forward followed by two steps back.

Oddly, in the past decade, the Romanian economy has performed in a "counter-cyclical" manner—that is, it has moved in the opposite direction to most of the rest of the world. Thus, in the boom years of the mid- to late 1990s, Romania endured a punishing internal recession that was little improved by whatever policies the government sought to implement. But more recently, in the 2000 to 2002 period, as the global economy slipped into its own recession, things seemed to be perking up in Romania, even as the government was changing hands.

However, the recent improvements are so far mostly of a macroeconomic nature, such as growth in gross domestic product (GDP). These sorts of measurements impress the country's international creditors, particularly the International Monetary Fund (IMF) and World Bank. But what does that mean to the average Romanian? Two telling statistics answer that question quickly: in 2001, 40 percent of the people were living on less than one dollar a day, and more than half of those polled believed their lives were better under Nicolae Ceauşescu's rule.

Why, more than a decade after the revolution, is life still so difficult in Romania for so many of its people?

Transforming a dysfunctional state-run economy into something resembling normal human exchange has proven complicated every-where. In Romania it was made harder. Whereas other late-era Com-munist rulers tried to buy off their subjects with consumer goods obtained through foreign loans, under Ceauşescu the "shock therapy" advocated after 1989 in Poland and elsewhere had already been applied for a decade, for perverse ends. Romanians were so poor they had no belts left to tighten.

Nonetheless, tighten them they did—they had no choice in the matter. While not instituting full "shock therapy" of the sort seen earlier in both Poland and Russia, both the leftist government of Ion Iliescu in 1990–96 and the rightist government of Emil Constantinescu in 1996–2000 at various times followed economic policies that severely hurt the bulk of the population, though in theory for their own long-term good.

Romania's dilemma was similar to that faced by many former commu-nist as well as Third World countries trying to integrate their economies into the free market model championed by the United States and Euro-pean Union (EU) in hopes of creating new jobs by direct foreign invest-ment. But first Romania had to satisfy the demands of the IMF to obtain multimillion-dollar loans to prop up the economy.

Between 1991 and 1994, under the first Iliescu regime, the govern-ment began implementing policies of "price liberalization"—subsidies that kept the price of basic goods and services artificially low were elimi-nated. The result was that the costs of food, fuel, electricity, and trans-portation rose as much as four or five times, prompting widespread social unrest, including waves of strikes and demonstrations. The same pattern was repeated in early 1997 under Constantinescu, when Premier Victor Ciorbea's government again lifted price controls, causing the cost of var-ious staples to jump as much four times.

At the same time that prices were skyrocketing, the value of the money in Romanians' pockets continued to lose value due to ravenous inflation that rose and fell in response to the government's monetary policies and other factors. Inflation peaked at a mind-boggling 292 percent in 1993, fell to 28 percent in 1995, rose to 57 percent in 1996, and shot up again to 155 percent in 1997. It slipped to 59 percent in 1998, 45 percent in 1999–2000, and 35 percent in 2001. The worst is apparently over, with inflation falling below 20 percent in 2002 and forecast at 14 percent in 2003.

As a result, the country's currency, the leu ("lion"; plural, lei) fell sharply during the 1990s. To put things in perspective, while it was considered a significant "psychological threshold" in 1993 when the leu reached the level of 1,000 to the U.S. dollar on the official exchange rate, in the 2001–2002 period it has averaged around 30,000 to the dollar!

Throughout this period, Romania continued to receive standby loans from the International Monetary Fund (IMF): $430 million in 1997, $547 million in 1999, and $380 million in 2001. Each loan was doled in a start-and-stop manner, punctuated by negotiations, with Romanian officials having to agree to eliminate remaining subsidies, cut the number and salaries of government employees, speed up privatization, and reduce the budget deficit to below 3.5 percent of GDP. The country was further aided in recent years by an annual influx of $600 million from the EU and nearly $1 billion from Romanians working abroad.

"Romania is probably the most advised country in the region," a foreign investment banker said in 2001. "Everyone knows what must be done. But does Romania have the political will to do it? Doubts persist."

Will or not, the country's luck seems to be turning. After suffering a negative growth rate throughout the 1990s, Romania's GDP jumped to a positive 5 percent in 2001 and 4.4 percent in 2002, among the highest growth rates in the region. The real question is when the benefits of those big numbers will begin to trickle down to the little guy in the Romanian street.

By the Numbers

The Romanian economy has also undergone a wrenching structural transformation in the years since the 1989 revolution. The country passed from an obsolete Soviet-style model based on heavy industry and collective agriculture to the new, post-industrial world of the service economy. More and more people work in jobs that don't produce material goods but rather provide services. The numbers are startling: the portion of GDP generated by service jobs had soared from around 20 percent at the start of the 1990s to an estimated 55–60 percent in 2000.

Conversely, industry's share of GDP has plunged from around 57 percent in 1989 to below 30 percent in 2000. Textiles, footwear, light machinery, and auto assembly have taken a greater share of the manufacturing sector compared to the more traditional industries of iron and steel making, heavy machinery, chemicals, and timber processing. Coal, iron ore, and salt are the major mining products. Onshore petroleum production has continued to decline, although it has been partially supplemented by new offshore platforms in the Black Sea. The strapped energy sector depends on oil, natural gas, coal, and hydroelectric power. Plans for Romania's first nuclear plant have been put on indefinite hold.

Agriculture has also lost ground, but to a lesser degree, going from about 22 percent to 14 percent of GDP over the past decade. The principal crops are wheat, corn (maize), barley, sugar beets, potatoes, sunflower seeds, grapes, cabbages, tomatoes, eggs, and lamb. Wine production, forestry, and fisheries remain mainstays as well.

The country's main source of imports and market for exports through 1991 was the Soviet Union. The dissolution in that year of both the USSR and the Soviet-dominated Council for Mutual Economic Assistance (CMEA, or Comecon) put a major crimp in Romania's balance-of-trade situation. But after a slow start, in recent years trade with the West has gathered pace: in 2001, 68 percent of Romanian exports went to the European Union and 57 percent of imports came from the EU. The top trading partners were Italy, Germany, France, Russia, and Turkey.

Romania's official unemployment rate has continued to hover around 10 percent, although the figure of the "underemployed"—those who don't work enough or earn enough to adequately support themselves—is clearly higher. Observers also note that the unofficial, or "informal," sector of the economy (which includes everything from untaxed, off-the-books labor, to barter, to black-market activity) is positively vast. Estimates of the informal economy's contribution to the GDP range from 30 to 50 percent, much of it in the service sector.

Government efforts to combat this trend have been proved to be problematic. In August 2000, for example, Bucharest Mayor Traian Basescu went on the offensive and ordered the removal of unlicensed and illegal kiosks from the streets of the capital city, sparking protests and violence. While presented as an attempt to stamp out corruption and

A woman worker wears a gas mask during a break from her job at a nonferrous metals plant in Copsa Mica. Some 300,000 tons of aerial pollutants pour out of the town's two factories each year, among the worst rates in Eastern Europe. (AP/Wide World Photos)

crime, "in effect, he sanctioned the destruction of the livelihoods of many Romanians and sent them to join the masses of the poverty-stricken."

Privatization: A Mixed Record

After the 1989 revolution, international humanitarian aid poured into Romania. But Western governments, banks, and businesses made it clear that large-scale financial aid and foreign investment for Romania would depend on the country completely restructuring its state-run command economy into a free market economy with large-scale private ownership. With support from the IMF, the World Bank, and other major lenders, the government established the National Agency for Privatization in August 1990 and enacted further laws in 1991 calling for the sell-off of state-owned enterprises to be completed within seven years.

In the six years that followed, however, the privatization program proceeded at a pace that can charitably be called glacial and that lagged far behind the rest of Eastern Europe. As one senior official put it, "Reform in Romania continually starts off in spring and dies off in autumn with the cold weather, when it falls back into the paralyzing sleep of hibernation."

There were a number of reasons for the delays. The cadres of state managers and bureaucrats, the so-called *nomenklatura,* competed for control of the privatization drive. Most of them had little incentive to speed up the process, which might result in their losing influence or even their jobs. In addition, the Iliescu government was accused of creating new bureaucratic hurdles to privatization under the excuse of streamlining the process. His party depended on the support of the *nomenklatura* and the votes of workers in state-run factories. Many economically nonviable plants would be closed, resulting in massive layoffs if privatization went ahead.

"The government is slow on privatization because it represents the big industries," according to Dan Pascariu, chairman of the Romanian Bank of Commerce. "The government still thinks of restructuring as a political concept rather than an economic or business one."

The government's fear of offending key industrial sector workers was not without basis. The coal miners from the Jiu Valley marched on Bucharest numerous times in the 1990s, as documented in the previous chapter. The uneconomical mining operations received heavy government subsidies, and the miners are among Romania's best-paid workers.

The Iliescu government dragged its feet on reform issues and this became a key reason for Constantinescu's victory in 1996. The pace of privatization indeed picked up from 1997 onward. Although it slowed down again after the reelection of Iliescu in 2000, by the government's figures more than 7,000 state-owned companies had been sold to private investors in the period of 1990–2001. However, many of these were small or medium-sized businesses, and the approximately 600 companies that remained to be privatized included a core group of large, money-losing industrial, manufacturing, and mining concerns that continue to drain the state's budget.

And whichever government was in power, many foreign investors continued to stay away because of bureaucratic hurdles and the high level of perceived corruption in Romania, which significantly raised the cost of doing business there. A nonprofit group called Transparency International ranked Romania 69th out of 91 countries in its 2001 Corruption Perception Index. (Neighboring Hungary came in at 31, while Bulgaria scored a 47.)

Unlike the industrial sector, the nation's agricultural system did undergo significant privatization in the 1990s. However, the reforms did not achieve as much success in increasing production as had been antic-ipated. Indeed, by the end of 1992, Romania—one of the most fertile countries in Europe—had reached the "embarrassing" point of having to import much of its food, according to its minister of agriculture. There were numerous reasons for the slow progress: Legal uncertainties contin-ued to deter new investment; fragmented land redistribution led to inef-ficient farming practices; and there was a persistent shortage of machinery and labor.

Under communism, the government ran 95 percent of all farming activity. It was divided between large state-run farms and smaller cooper-atives, both of which had access to machine and tractor stations and a single supply and distribution network. After the revolution, members of the cooperatives were given provisional ownership certificates and offered various options regarding how they wished to farm.

By 2000, more than 80 percent of farmlands were in private hands, but the practice still remained very labor-intensive due to a lack of mod-ern equipment. (While making up less than 20 percent of GDP, agricul-ture employs 40 percent of Romania's workforce.) Many farmers are forced to use horses instead of tractors both for plowing and getting their produce to market. The following scene from the mid-1990s remains a typical one in 21st-century Romania:

> Along the 100 miles from Artand on the Hungarian border to Cluj farmers could be seen cutting and stacking hay and hauling it to their barns. No one was using machinery, just scythes and wooden pitch-forks—pastoral, picturesque and utterly pre-industrial . . . Not a sin-gle tractor was seen along the Artand-Cluj road.

Another problem is the growing labor shortage, as the long-term migration of young people from rural to urban areas continues. One sur-vey of more than 500 villages found that 59 percent of Romania's farm workers are now over 60 years old, while only 8.9 percent are under 40.

The government is open to admitting the problems and trying to devise solutions. So far, it has sought most of all to keep the price of agri-cultural production under control to protect urban consumers. But 45 percent of the population still live in rural areas, and there is a growing recognition in Bucharest that the urban-rural balance now has to be shifted back in favor of the farmers if the potentially great riches of Romanian agriculture are to be realized.

The Caritas Scheme

One of the more amazing economic stories of post-revolutionary Romania revolves around the so-called Caritas Affair. Caritas began as a "mutual aid" society in the Transylvanian city of Brașov and then moved its operations to Cluj in June 1992. Devised by an accountant, Ioan Stoica, it promised investors an eightfold return on their money within three months. It thus appeared to be a classic pyramid scheme (also known as a Ponzi scheme), in which the money of new investors is used to pay back earlier investors rather than for any legitimate money-making enterprise. But the supply of funds cannot rise exponentially forever, and eventually all such scams collapse of their own weight, leaving the early investors rich and the later ones bankrupt.

Many Romanians, confronted with high inflation and low bank interest rates, cared little about such matters. In the first nine months of 1993, despite warnings from the government, an estimated 3 million to 4 million Romanians (a fifth of the adult population) invested $1 billion in the get-rich-quick scheme, a sum equal to half of the government's annual budget. Thousands of people from around the country descended on Cluj in what was termed "mass psychosis," "chaos," and "a new El Dorado."

Aside from Stoica and other early investors, many of whom became millionaires, the other main beneficiary was Gheorghe Funar, mayor of Cluj and leader of the extremist Party of Romanian National Unity (PRNU), who was an early and ardent backer of Caritas. As a result, his city and party received a huge influx of funds as well as massive media attention, all of which served Funar's ambitions to expand the PRNU from its Transylvanian base into a truly national party.

Caritas failed to pay out substantial returns to investors from November 1993 onward. But predictions of a social explosion in the wake of the scheme's gradual collapse proved unfounded. Many investors reportedly blamed the failure on the government, the central bank, and the news media rather than on Stoica or Funar. (Stoica was finally arrested in August 1994.)

Many observers were surprised that the scam lasted as long as it did. Speculation swirled as to who or what provided the "deep pockets" behind Caritas, which some suspected was in fact a gigantic, criminal money-laundering operation (in which "dirty" money is "cleaned" by being cycled through legitimate channels). The possible culprits mentioned in Romanian news accounts included the Romanian Intelligence Service (RIS), the Italian Mafia, or Eastern European organized crime gangs. Some suggested that the money behind Caritas originated from international drug-trafficking or illegal arms sales to various sides of the Yugoslavian civil wars.

Sadly, the same pattern repeated itself seven years later, but this time with a financial concern that on the surface appeared to be more legitimate than the notorious Caritas. It was a high-interest earning trust company called the National Investment Fund, which collapsed in May 2000 amid charges that its directors had embezzled huge sums of money from investors. Once again, many hard-working Romanians lost their life savings. Rumors also spread that the Banc Commerciala Romana and BANCOREX—the largest banks in Romania—were running short of cash, and the National Bank of Romania had to step in to prevent their complete collapse.

Dracula Tourism

It says a lot about the state of Romania's moribund economy that one of the most highly touted recent ideas for bringing in foreign dollars involves capitalizing on the legend of the dead coming back to life—that is to say, "Dracula tourism."

The impetus for the initiative was the fact that, despite the country's considerable tourism potential, it has failed to attract foreign visitors in significant numbers because of lack of promotion and Western-style infrastructure (such as modern hotels), largely due to inadequate investment. Only three million foreigners visited Romania in 2000, as compared to 15 million in the neighboring, and much smaller, Hungary.

In an ambitious bid to turn things around, Tourism Minister Dan Agathon in November 2001 announced plans to build a family-style Dracula theme park on a 130-hectare plot near the town of Sighişoara in

THE COCA-COLA REVOLUTION

The Coca-Cola Company provided one of the brightest spots in the Romanian economy during the early transition period. In early 1990 it became one of the first foreign firms to invest in the country. By the beginning of 1995, Coke had invested a total of $150 million (out of a total of $1.5 billion in Eastern Europe) to create local bottlers and a sales and distribution system for its famous soft drink. In a three-year period Romanians went from drinking no Coke to an average of 47 eight-ounce servings a year, the fastest growth rate in company history.

More importantly, a study by an American business college found that "a minimum of 23,900 jobs was supported by the sale of Coca-Cola products in the Romanian retail sector." For each job that Coke created directly, 11 jobs were created elsewhere in the economy, and "as many as 20,000 to 25,000 kiosks and other small retail shops started or maintained their business because of Coca-Cola." This was helping to form a base for free-market activity and to create a new class of small-scale entrepreneurs—the hated "petty bourgeoisie" of Marxist jargon.

"Our system always guaranteed that we got second-rate products, so there was no pride in what we sold," one storekeeper says. "Then Coke comes in with its new trucks and new bottles and its drivers in new uniforms. Everything is high quality. That makes us feel better about ourselves."

Romanians do not seem to suffer from the fear of "Coca-colonization" at the hands of multinational corporations that is common in some foreign countries. "There is not the feeling in Romania of being exploited by multinationals," according to a government economist. "Rather, people see multinationals as a vehicle for transferring organizational and managerial skills."

WINE BEFORE ITS TIME
A less inspiring story involves an indigenous Romanian beverage: wine. Romanians consume an average of more than 40 bottles per person annually, twice the rate of Britain. The country has one of the best climates in the world for wine-growing, and some of its vintages are

central Transylvania. It would feature a scary castle with spooky effects and mock torture chambers surrounded by amusement rides, a maze garden, restaurants serving "scary meat jelly," and a semi-serious interna-

world famous. Romania is the world's eighth-largest wine producer—making 600 million liters (150 million gallons) a year—but exports only four percent of that total. By comparison, post-Communist Hungary exports 40 percent of its wine production, while Bulgaria exports 70 percent.

One problem is that, although most Romanian vineyards are now privately owned, they lack the capital and foreign investment needed for expansion. That may change, but not soon enough to suit the nation's winegrowers. "We are in a transition period from a very stupid government to a medium-stupid government," says Viorel Stoian, head of the National Wine Institute. "Meanwhile, our vineyards are deteriorating."

Wine tasting facilities in a winery in Murfatlar that has been helped by UN development aid. Murfatlar is the most important wine region on Romania's Black Sea coast. (UN photo 177419/M. Grant)

tional center for "vampirology," the study of vampires. The "simple and suggestive" slogan for the park coined by advertising experts: "Welcome Forever."

The idea was boosted by the success of director Francis Ford Coppola's 1992 Hollywood blockbuster *Dracula*, which melded Bram Stoker classic fictional creation together with the bloody history of Romania's 15th-century prince-tyrant Vlad Tepes, also known as Vlad the Impaler. (See Chapter 2.) But because U.S.-based Universal Studios owned the copyright on the now-famous caped visage of Count Dracula popularized by actor Bela Lugosi in the original movies from the 1930s and 1940s, Romanian planners would have to come up with a new, home-grown appearance for the vampire.

"We can't compete with Austria's ski resorts," said one tourism official. "But Dracula is unique to us. We don't even have to explain what it means, so we save money with advertising."

The number three seemed to figure strongly in the projections for the park: it would cost $30 million to build, generate $3 million a year in profits, attract 3,000 visitors a day, and create 3,000 jobs. Nevertheless, the plans ironically generated stiff opposition from environmentalists and other civic groups in Sighişoara (which, perhaps not accidentally, was the birthplace of Vlad Tepes). They complained that the park would be built on the site of the country's oldest oak forest, and that development and the influx of tourists would harm the historic character of the old town, whose 13th-century center has been designated as a World Heritage Site by the U.N.

Despite the outcry, officials pushed ahead, and in April 2002 Agathon announced that investors had bought $2.9 million worth of nearly $5 million in stock that was offered in the project. But opposition persisted, and in early 2003, PricewaterhouseCoopers—a Western consulting firm hired by Romania to conduct a financial feasibility study—advised the government not to build the park in Sighişoara. Instead, they suggested it be located in a more accessible location, such as Bucharest or a Black Sea resort.

Like its namesake, the planned park will be hard to kill off. In the meantime, it generated almost as many stories in the Western press as Romania's bid to join NATO. (It also provided a field day for headline writers: "Dracula Park Expected to Pump Fresh Blood Into Ailing Tourism Industry," "Investors' Stakes Give Life to Dracula," and "Perhaps No Home Soil for Dracula," to cite just a few.)

And in perhaps the greatest irony of all, it turns out that the late Nicolae Ceauşescu has proven a greater tourist draw than the Prince of Darkness himself, bringing in 10 times as much revenue as that generated by vampire fans. "Foreigners with a taste for the macabre are flocking to attractions linked to Ceauşescu, even though the country has done virtually nothing to promote what is now being described as 'dictator tourism.'" Favored sites include palaces and hunting lodges they frequented and the Targoviste military base where Ceauşescu and his wife Elena were executed.

"It's amazing," said Agathon. "We spent a lot of the ministry's budget on ideas like the Dracula theme park . . . Now, without even trying, we find that people are interested in every aspect of Ceauşescu's life, and thousands of private operators are catering to this demand."

And it's not only foreign tourists who are visiting the dictator's old haunts—some Romanians, nostalgic for what they view as the good old days, are doing the same. Says 64-year-old Dumitra Popu: "Ceauşescu didn't need characters like Dracula to bring foreign tourists here, and I can tell you there were more people coming in those days than now."

NOTES

p. 116 "'Transforming a dysfunctional state-run economy . . .'" Tony Judt, *The New York Review of Books,* November 1, 2001.

p. 117 "'Romania is probably the most advised country . . .'" Steve Erlanger, *New York Times,* February 11, 2001.

p. 119 "'in effect, he sanctioned the destruction . . .'" Catherine Lovatt. "Nations in Transit 2001: Romania.'" Available on-line. URL: http://www.freedomhouse. org/research/nattransit.htm. Downloaded on October 12, 2002.

p. 119 " 'Reform in Romania continually starts off . . .' " Don Ionescu, *Transition,* April 14, 1995.

p. 120 "'The government is slow on privatization . . .'" Ionescu.

p. 121 "reached the 'embarrassing' point of having . . ." David C. Henry, *RFE/RL,* February 18, 1994.

p. 121 "'Along the 100 miles from Artand . . .'" David B. Ottaway, *Washington Post,* August 1, 1994.

p. 122 "'mass psychosis . . . chaos . . .'" Michael Shafir, *RFE/RL,* September 24, 1993.

p. 124 "'a minimum of 23,900 jobs . . .'" Nathaniel C. Nash, *New York Times,* February 26, 1995.

pp. 124–125 "'scary meat jelly . . . vampirology . . .'" Eugen Tomiuc, "Romania: Dracula Park Expected to Pump Fresh Blood Into Ailing Tourism Industry,"

RFE/RL. Available on-line. URL: http://www.rferl.org/nca/features/2001/11/0811200182145.asp. Posted on Nov. 11, 2001.

p. 125 " 'We are in a transition period . . .'" Nathaniel C. Nash, *New York Times*, March 8, 1995.

p. 126 "'We can't compete with Austria's . . .'" Tom Zeller, "Hold the Bloody Mary," *New York Times*. Available on-line. URL: http://www.nytimes.com/2002/0.../26ZELL.html. Posted on May 26, 2002.

p. 127 " 'Foreigners with a taste for the macabre . . .' " Ed Holt, "Ceaușescu Beats Dracula to Bring New Blood into Romanian Tourism," *Scotland on Sunday*. Available on-line. URL: http://www.scotlandonsunday.com/international.cfm?id=1422262002. Posted on December 22, 2002.

p. 127 " 'It's amazing, . . .'" Holt. "Ceaușescu Beats Dracula . . ."

p. 127 "'Ceaușescu didn't need characters . . .'" Holt. "Ceaușescu Beats Dracula . . ."

9

DAILY LIFE

The transition to democracy and a free-market economy has remained a rough road for most Romanians. There is no doubt that the new political freedoms and the ending of the most totalitarian aspects of communism under Ceauşescu—such as the constant surveillance by the Securitate and the ban on abortions and birth control—have made daily life less psychologically oppressive and easier to bear. But most Romanians, like people all over the world, are preoccupied with day-to-day concerns: safe streets, decent housing, health care, and feeding their families. By these basic yardsticks, the quality of life in Romania has shown no improvement, an actual regression or only a marginal advantage since the 1989 revolution.

And public opinion surveys over the years have consistently shown that, aside from the wealthy and upper-middle class elite, most Romanians are tired of a transition that never seems to end, or even go anywhere. Free elections and the chance to join NATO appear to have done little to concretely improve many people's lives, leaving both left- and right-wing governments to face a significant minority (particularly among the elderly) who are actually nostalgic for the communist era.

Winters remain the hardest time of year. The government is sensitive to comparisons of the present period to the notorious "Ceauşescu winters" of the 1980s, when the heat was often turned off and people froze in their dimly lit apartments. While things are not quite so bad, today the question is usually not an absence of heat but the lack of money to pay for it.

On paper, Romania has a comprehensive social welfare system. Government- and employer-funded insurance schemes provide for health care, sickness benefits, children's allowances, unemployment payments, and pensions. But such benefits, even where they actually exist, were not adequate to cope with the huge price increases in basic goods and services that occurred throughout the 1990s as various governments ended many subsidies on everything from fuel to food.

Housing remains a major problem. Under Ceaușescu, the government built dreary high-rise apartment complexes for workers in urban areas. Most of these were shoddily built and have not aged well, but none of the post-Communist governments have had the funds to replace them and the struggling free market in construction has not taken up the slack.

A 2002 report by the UN Economic Commission for Europe doesn't mince words: "Ten years of transition in Romania have not brought about an improvement in average living conditions. In general, Romanians still live in cramped housing and only half have access to piped water . . . The quality of rural homes in particularly poor . . . a family of eight is more likely to live in a two-room flat than in a home with four rooms or more."

On a brighter note, the report noted that a new public housing construction program was begun in 2000 with international financing. Meanwhile, U.S.-based charity Habitat for Humanity has also done work in Romania. One project was building a new home in Beius for Adrian and Mihaela Tapos, both medical doctors who had previously lived with their four children in an apartment intended to temporarily house single doctors. With no running water or bathroom facilities, Mihaela recalls, life wasn't easy: "We had to carry the water from a pit well, and then pour it in the big 200-liter barrel in the loft," she said. "Water was pulled out of the well with a long wood stick that had a metal pick at the end to hold the water handle. We did this for five years."

As in many other places, life in Romania is particularly hard for women, whatever their profession. Trafficking in women for the purpose of forced prostitution is a growing problem, both inside the country and internationally. The prosecution of rape is also difficult because it requires both a medical certificate and a witness, and a rapist can avoid punishment if he marries the victim.

Domestic violence is common, though many men fail to recognize it as a problem. The April 2000 issue of the Romanian edition of *Playboy* magazine included a "satirical" article explaining in graphic detail how to beat one's wife without leaving marks. International and domestic protests led to apologies by *Playboy*'s foreign editors and local publisher, and prompted a follow-up article on the costs of domestic violence.

The Health Crisis

An even more telling example of the Ceauşescu legacy is demonstrated by Romania's continuing health care crisis. By most statistical indicators the situation has gotten steadily worse since the 1989 revolution, a reflection of both the stagnant economy and "health hazards accumulated during the communist era." These include environmental pollution, a shortage of medicines, and unheated homes in winter.

In 1992 the nation's population actually decreased by 3,462, the first time that had happened in modern Romanian history outside of wartime, and a process that continued in the year that followed. (The population declined an estimated 0.21 percent in 2002.) Two major factors were increased emigration and the ending of Ceauşescu's "pro-birth" policies, which had banned abortion and contraceptives. The end of those restrictions caused the ratio of abortions to births to explode: It was three to one in 1990–91, one of the highest such rates in the world. The introduction of more progressive, Western family-planning practices lowered the ratio to just over 1 to 1 by 1998.

Life expectancy in Romania is among the lowest in Europe: 69.5 years in 2002 (74 for women; 67 for men), down from 71 in 1989. From 1991 to 2002 the death rate per 1,000 inhabitants rose from 10.9 to 12.3, while the birth rate fell from 11.9 to 10.8. The infant mortality rate (measuring the number of babies who die before their first birthday), after reaching 23.4 deaths per 1,000 infants in 1992, fell but remained high at 19 in 2002. This rate in Europe is second only to Albania's. (The average rate for Europe, including former Communist countries, was just over 10 per 1,000.)

Various communicable diseases are also on the rise. Tuberculosis—known as the "squalor disease" because it is spread by unsanitary living conditions—climbed steadily from 64 people per 1,000 in 1990 to 116 in

1999. Contaminated drinking water has caused increasingly frequent epidemics of hepatitis A, while between 8 percent and 10 percent of Romanians are believed to carry the virus for hepatitis B, which, like AIDS, is spread by contaminated blood transfusions, syringes, and unprotected sex.

THE ORPHAN STORY

Romanians are a proud people, and so they often find themselves discouraged and embarrassed that the only thing many Americans seem to know about their country (aside from vampire stories) is the sad tale of its orphans. Perhaps that is not too surprising, because—as one scholar has written—"The discovery after 1989 of orphanages filled with thousands of wretched children living in medieval filth was the single most horrible revelation to come out of any formerly communist country in Eastern Europe."

Many of these children were not technically orphans, for they had been abandoned after their mothers were forced to give birth to them (Ceaușescu having banned abortions and contraception in a mad effort to increase the population). It was subsequently discovered that as many as one baby in every four was infected with AIDS due to contaminated blood injections. The orphans' plight was widely publicized in the West, and many foreign couples traveled to Romania in the immediate aftermath of the revolution to arrange quick, if legally questionable, adoptions.

One traveler who visited an orphanage in the early 1990s wrote movingly of being surrounded by children as she left: "'When will my mother come? Whose mother are you?' they keep asking. One of them puts his arm through mine, and walks with me toward the gate with the look of the purest sadness and supplication I've ever seen in human eyes."

But where many saw a tragedy, others saw an ongoing opportunity, and Romania proceeded to supply two-thirds of all international adoptions in the world in the 1990s. The European Parliament eventually condemned the practice as a "profitable trade in child trafficking," and the European Union demanded a moratorium. In October 2001, the government banned international adoptions for a year, and later extended the ban into 2003.

The ban put Romania and the EU at odds with the U.S. government, which sided with American and other couples trying to

As of 1999, the government had estimated that 7,000 cases of AIDS existed in Romania.

Romania has more than 49,000 doctors (including 6,500 dentists), making for a ratio of one practicing physician for every 580 people—not

adopt, though President Ion Iliescu was unsympathetic. "Americans should produce their own children," he said. "Our main goal is to improve conditions for all children in our country." According to Premier Adrian Nastase, "adoption was an area with a lot of corruption," with Romanian orphans selling on the Internet for up to $50,000.

Meanwhile, international aid was helping to improve the quality of the facilities and caregiving at orphanages, government officials said, and the number of institutionalized children had fallen to about 43,000 from the 100,000 of Ceauşescu's day.

One of the poignant images of Romania's orphans that gripped the world's attention in the early 1990s. (AP/Wide World Photos)

an impressive statistic. Medical professionals are also seriously underpaid, prompting many to emigrate abroad. Other problems in the health care system include the poor physical state of the nation's hospitals and clinics, and an antiquated pharmaceutical industry.

Romania's government appears to have insufficient resources to confront the crisis. Health care costs took up 5 percent of the country's gross domestic product in 2000. Privatization plays a major role in the government's plans for health care reform, but so far the country's pharmacies are the only sector to have been extensively privatized.

Because doctors are so poorly paid, most patients (assuming they can afford it) accept that they must supplement their salaries with informal fees or gifts. "But the real bribes kick in when a Romanian goes to the hospital," according to one account. "There 'you need to bribe everyone,' says one Romanian man who has just gone through the experience. To get a Caesarean operation for his pregnant wife, he had to pay a total of $200 for the surgeon, nurses, and food for one week. That sum of money is out of the reach of many average Romanians."

Finally, it is widely agreed that the persistence of pollution remains one of Romania's most serious public health problems. As one observer noted, "Communism was an ecological disaster everywhere, but in Romania its mess has proven harder to clean up." There, the issue is most commonly thought of in terms of how airborne particles and gases affect people's breathing in places like Zlatna, a town long infamous for its chronic air pollution from smelter emissions.

But in 2000, a singular event occurred in a different medium— water—that was so devastating some called it Europe's worst ecological disaster since the 1986 Chernobyl nuclear accident in Ukraine. On January 30 in Transylvania, heavy rains and snow caused a basin at the Aurul gold mine operation, which contained cyanide and other toxic substances used in extracting gold, to overflow into the Szamos River. An estimated 22 million gallons of deadly sludge flowed into Hungary's Tisza River in the two weeks that followed, and from there into the mighty Danube.

Up to 90 percent of the aquatic life in the worst-affected areas was killed, producing an estimated 220,000 pounds (100,000 kilograms) of dead fish. There were no immediate reported human casualties, and the flowing water eventually diluted the poisons to acceptable levels, but the long-term impact of the disaster remains unknown. The responsible party, Aurul, was a joint venture of the Romanian government and an Australian company, Esmeralda Exploration Ltd. In a telling comment on the state of affairs in Romania today, each side denied any responsibility and blamed the other.

NOTES

p. 130 "'Ten years of transition in Romania . . .'" United Nations Economic Commission for Europe. "Housing Market Alone Cannot Accommodate All Romanians." Country profile issued on April 9, 2002. Available on-line. URL: http://www.un.ro/English-hm.doc.

p. 130 "'We had to carry the water . . .'" Habitat World. "Habitat House Yields Stability." The Publication of Habitat for Humanity International, April–May 2002. Available on-line. URL: http://www.habitat.org/hw/april-may02/feature_7.html.

p. 131 "The April 2000 issue of the Romanian edition . . ." U.S. Department of State. "Romania: Country Reports on Human Rights Practices — 2000." Released February 23, 2001. Available on-line. URL: http://www.state.gov/g/drl/rls/hrrpt/2000/eur/881.htm.

p. 131 "'health hazards accumulated during the communist era.'" Don Ionescu, *RFE/RL*, October 8, 1993.

p. 132 "'The discovery after 1989 of orphanages . . .'" Gale Stokes, *The Walls Came Tumbling Down*, p. 58.

p. 132 "'When will my mother come? . . .'" Eva Hoffman, *Exit into History: A Journey Through the New Eastern Europe*, p. 329.

p. 133 "'Americans should produce their own children . . .'" Danica Kirka, *Miami Herald*. Available on-line. URL: http://www.miami.com/mld/miamiherald/news/world/4831391.htm. Posted on December 29, 2002.

p. 134 "'But the real bribes kick in . . .'" Kitty McKinsey. "Bulgaria/Romania: A Study of Two Failing Health-Care Systems." *RFE/RL*. Available on-line. URL: http://www.rferl.org/nca/features/1997/05/F.RU.97052090817.html. Downloaded on February 3, 2003.

p. 134 "'Communism was an ecological disaster everywhere . . .'" Tony Judt, *The New York Review of Books*, November 1, 2001.

10
ARTS & CULTURE

For a nation of relatively small size, Romania has an impressive artistic and cultural heritage. All Romanians, from the humblest peasant to the most elite intellectual, take great pride in that achievement. In the words of musician Georges Enesco: "If only our administration and politics were on the same level as the arts, we would be one of the happiest countries on earth."

Romania is also a well-educated country, in the sciences as well as the arts. The oldest school in the country, located at the monastery in Cenadul Vechi, dates from the 11th century. Today there are 48 institutions of higher learning (with 186 colleges), including 13 full universities, four technological universities, and many private institutes. The prior Communist regimes—although they tried to indoctrinate students with Marxist dogma—did provide free, universal, and compulsory education, and virtually eradicated illiteracy. (Today only 2.6 percent of the population 12 and older cannot read or write.) In the 1990s the educational system was reorganized to eliminate mandatory ideological training.

Shortly after the 1989 revolution, one writer noted: "Whoever talked to the new breed of Romanian students came away amazed by the breadth of their vision despite years of school-room indoctrination, by their courage, and by their language, refreshingly free of cant and the remnants of Marxist-Leninist cliches."

The Communist era did have a significant, damaging impact on Romania's artistic and intellectual community. Only a few of its members were brave enough to become open dissidents during the Ceauşescu dictatorship. Some went quietly into exile while most stayed behind to become either open or tacit collaborators with the regime. After the revolution, the dissident poet Mircea Dinescu was asked by a foreign journalist why the Romanian Writers' Union did not hold a tribunal to pass judgment on those members who had served as apologists for the Ceauşescus. "But Madame," he replied, "that is half the entire Union and there are some very good writers among them."

Although the dictator's wife Elena was widely viewed as a cruel, spiteful, and ignorant woman, Romania's leading intellectuals had to publicly pretend to believe the mythology that she was a world-class thinker and scientist. In some respects she became even more hated than her husband because of the baleful and repressive influence she wielded over the country's intellectual climate:

> Elena Ceauşescu added a special poison, and it may be said that her bequest to the country was a traumatized intelligentsia. Asked after the revolution to explain her, a young writer could only mutter that it was impossible to understand how such a woman had existed in the twentieth century.

In a similar vein, the former diplomat Mircea Codreanu asserted that had Elena lived, she should have been tried "for genocide not of people but of culture and education."

Art, Music, and Literature

Up until the 19th century, the creation of art in Romania was exclusively a religious occupation. This process reached its high point with the famous 15th- and 16th-century painted Orthodox churches and monasteries of Bukovina, in northern Moldavia, the exterior surfaces of which are decorated with beautiful frescoes illustrating Bible stories for the peasant faithful. In the modern period, however, Romania's most famous painters (who include Nicolae Grigorescu, Theodor Aman, Alexandru Ciucurencu, and Ion Tuculescu) have taken that heritage of folk and monastic art and combined it with more modern European motifs.

A statue (The Kiss) *by Constantin Brancusi (1876–1957), considered one of the greatest sculptors of the modern era. Today most of his works are on display in France and the United States.* (Courtesy Library of Congress)

Romania's most famous artist is Constantin Brancusi (1876–1957), one of the world's greatest sculptors. He was born in a village near Tirgu Jiu in the region of Oltenia. At the age of seven he worked as a shepherd in the Carpathians, and later went on to higher education in Bucharest. He immigrated to Paris in 1904, where he gained international fame as a fixture of the modern art movement, pioneering abstract techniques of reducing sculpture to its "pure form" or essence. Despite his modernism, Brancusi gained much of his initial inspiration from the Romanian folk art and myths he was exposed to in his youth. Today most of his masterpieces are on display in France and the United States, although there is a popular sculpture garden of his works in Tirgu Jiu.

Georges Enesco (1881–1955)—composer, violinist, pianist, conductor, and teacher—is easily Romania's greatest contribution to the world of music. He incorporated Gypsy melodies in his Romanian Rhapsodies, as well as composing three symphonies and an opera.

Romania's literature before World War I consisted primarily of ballads, folk tales, and poems. "The Romanian is born a poet," is a sentiment often expressed in Romania. Although underappreciated in his lifetime, Mikhai Eminescu is today considered the country's greatest 19th-century poet. Between World Wars I and II, a number of other poets achieved prominence, including George Bacovia, Tudor Arghezi, Ion Barbu, and

Adrian Maniu. Two novelists who also became widely known were Eugen Lovinescu and Titu Maiorescu.

The most famous figure of the postwar period was playwright Eugène Ionesco, who in the late 1950s became one of the leading figures of the so-called theater of the absurd, which mixed elements of tragedy, comedy, and surrealism. He died in March 1994 at the age of 81. Although he lived mostly in Paris and wrote in French, his world view was strongly shaped by the 13-year period he spent in Romania as a young man during its Fascist period. "The Ceauşescus were just the latest in a line of farcical figures who have held power in Romania," one Romanian has noted. "It's no accident . . . that Ionesco emerged from here. To him, theater of the absurd was merely theater of the real."

The Communist takeover brought a massive disruption in Romania's literary evolution as writers sought to cope with government censorship and restrictive Marxist views of art, problems that persisted for the next 40 years. Dumitru Radu Popescu became the most prominent writer of the 1960s, his novel *The Blue Lion* openly questioning the Communist regime. Among the few who openly stood up to Ceauşescu in the 1970s and 1980s were poets Dinescu and Anna Blandiana and writer Paul Goma. Poet Nina Cassian and writer Norman Manea made names for themselves after going into exile in the United States.

Mass Media Explosion

There is no better example of Romanians' hunger for knowledge than the virtual explosion of freedom that took place in the mass media—newspapers, magazines, book publishing, and television and radio—beginning immediately after the revolution. The country went from an extremely centralized state-run system, where the Communist Party exercised strict censorship over a handful of newspapers and broadcasters, to a broad array of outlets for information, entertainment, and culture.

Today, while state-owned Romania Television broadcasts on three channels and is still the most widely watched main TV station, and state-owned radio broadcasts on five different stations, both face a crowded and competitive market. The most popular privately owned stations are ProTV and Antena 1, which along with other smaller competitors broadcast 56 programs nationwide. Cable TV has made big inroads, with 2.8 million subscribers as of 2002, and the number of Internet users is estimated at 800,000.

The media sector is certainly the country's most successful example of privatization. The government no longer funds any print media, and instead of the 24 state-run publishing houses under Ceaușescu, there are now over 3,000 private publishers. Romania's biggest newspapers are *Adevarul, Romania Libera,* and *Evenimentul Zilei,* and the 15 national dailies had a combined circulation of 1.5 million in 2001.

Overall, while often politically biased, Romania's press continues to be open and lively. It energetically performs its role of the watchdog, exposing corruption scandals and other abuses of power.

Folk Culture

The folk art and folklore of Romania's peasant culture is among the richest and best preserved of Europe. Each region of the country has its own distinctive dress and crafts—including pottery, ceramics, rug-making, weaving, and woodcarving—as well as dancing and music. But even these ancient and enduring popular traditions were somewhat tainted by their use as standard props in government-sponsored propaganda exercises during the Ceaușescu era, as Andrei Codrescu found when he returned from exile:

> I looked back and saw, coming around a bend on the road, a wide peasant cart drawn by two sturdy horses. The cart was loaded full of hay, and two peasants in long sheepskin coats sat over it, holding their whips like batons over the clippity-clop of hooves on hard snow. They were almost unbearably picturesque, like fake peasants in a pseudofolk tableau. They lifted their caps as they passed. Ceaușescu's propaganda had made so much of the "peasant" that his reality was hard to fathom. One of the subtler crimes of nationalist propaganda is to make even the genuine unreal, to turn the world into postcard and caricature. One of the artistic tasks of the future will be to extract the peasant from the pseudopeasant, folk music from "folkloric ensembles," folk art from "popular socialist art."

A classic example of modern Romanian folk art: the "merry cemetery" in Sapanța, where carved headboards and humorous epitaphs commemorate the dead. (Courtesy Romanian National Tourist Office, New York)

No discussion of popular culture would be complete without a brief introduction to Romania's delicious and exotic national cuisine. There is *ciorba*, a sour soup made from fermented bran, bacon, potatoes, and beef or chicken. Hearty stews such as *tochitura moldoveneasca* are often accompanied by *mamaliga*, a maize polenta. *Sarmale* is a spicy dish of bitter cabbage leaves stuffed with meat, and *mititei* are small grilled sausages perfumed with aromatic herbs. Among fish dishes, carp on the spit is a local specialty in the Danube delta region. Pork is the meat most commonly served. Indeed, a recent travel writer found that at many Romanian restaurants, "the litany of specials can sound like a Monty Python routine ('Pork, pork, pork, pork, pork . . . and I think we might also have some pork left')."

Sports

Romania is a sports-mad country. Even in rural areas one can often see endless groups of amateur athletes in fashionable warm-up suits jogging along the roadside. Romania has produced its own share of international sports stars, such as tennis player Ilie Nastase. More recently, a Romanian basketball player—7-foot, 7-inch Gheorghe Muresan—was picked in the 1994 National Basketball Association draft to play professionally in the United States with the Washington Bullets. But when most people think of Romanian sports, they probably think of the dozens of Olympic gold medals its women's gymnastics teams have won over the years, beginning with the famous victory of Nadia Comaneci at the 1976 Olympic Games.

Nadia defected to the West shortly before the 1989 revolution. She quickly received bad press in the United States when she initially took up with a fellow Romanian escapee who turned out to be a married man, although the affair was short-lived. But she remained a national hero to most Romanians, a status that was reaffirmed when she made a triumphant return visit to Bucharest in 1995.

Another outpouring of national affection occurred the following year, when Nadia returned to Bucharest for her wedding to former U.S. gold medal–winning gymnast Bart Conner—a marriage of gymnastics royalty.

A more unfortunate moment for the sport occurred at the 2000 Summer Olympics, when Romania's Andreea Raducan was stripped

Gymnast Andreea Raducan of Romania competes on the floor during the 2000 Summer Olympic Games in Sydney.
(AP/Wide World Photos)

of the gold medal she won in the individual women's competition after she inadvertently took a cold medicine that contained traces of a banned substance. However, her fellow Romanian Simona Amanar then moved up to take the gold, and Raducan was allowed to keep the medal she won as part of Romania's gold-medal winning squad in the team competition.

However, as in many countries in the world, the biggest sport in Romania is soccer. That obsession grew even stronger in the wake of Romania's unexpected success at the 1994 World Cup, held in the United States. There Romania's national team, led by its star player Gheorghe Hagi, advanced to the quarterfinals only to lose to Sweden in a heartbreaker; after battling to a 2-2 tie, Sweden won 5-4 in the sudden death penalty kick shootout. For all the problems and divisions in Romanian society, the glorious near-triumph was a moment that brought the entire country together in joyous celebration.

NOTES

p. 137 "'If only our administration . . .'" Norman Manea, *On Clowns: The Dictator and the Artist*, p. 17.

p. 137 "'Whoever talked to the new breed . . .'" Edward Behr, *Kiss the Hand You Cannot Bite*, p. 278.

p. 138 "'But madame, . . .'" Mark Frankland, *The Patriots' Revolution*, p. 314.

p. 138 "'Elena Ceaușescu added a special poison . . .'" Frankland, p. 312.

p. 138 "'for genocide not of people but . . .'" Behr, p. 275.

p. 139 "'The Romanian is born a poet.'" Manea, p. 17.

p. 141 "'I looked back and saw . . .'" Andrei Codrescu, *The Hole in the Flag*, p. 151.

p. 142 "'Pork, pork, pork, pork, pork, pork . . .'" Jack Barth, *Travel & Leisure*, December 1994.

11

FOREIGN POLICY

For centuries, during periods of both subjugation and independence, Romanians have had a reputation for handling their foreign relations with far greater skill than their domestic affairs. It is a story that has continued in the post-communist era, when Romanian diplomats and military officers have gradually succeeded in forging strong links with Western Europe and the United States at a time when their country's economic backwardness would have otherwise left it isolated. Bucharest has played a particularly shrewd hand following the September 11, 2001, terrorist attacks on the United States, resulting in an invitation to join NATO and a visit by President George W. Bush a year later.

The process of cultivating international relations did not begin smoothly, however. In the 1990–92 period, the leading Western nations essentially put Romania on probation. They warned the new government in Bucharest that it would have to improve its domestic record on political and economic reforms and human rights if it wanted to join the international community as a member in good standing. Because of its slowness to make such necessary changes, Romania fell far behind the other formerly Communist countries of Eastern Europe in the amount of trade, aid, and investment it received from the West.

The new government really had only itself to blame, as Nestor Ratesh noted:

> In December 1989, Romania gained the world's affection as never before. It soon lost it. The power of the former Communists, the shadowy

presence of the security police, the political and ethnic violence, the rough treatment of the opposition, and the governmentcontrol of the radio and television all combined to undermine the postrevolutionary leadership's credibility abroad, especially in the West. In a few months, the precious capital of goodwill was mindlessly dissipated.

Many Romanians tended, as usual, to place the blame on outsiders rather than themselves. A leading Bucharest journalist exclaimed: "A new martyrdom begins for Romania. No sooner has the burden [of Ceauşescu] been lifted, albeit incompletely, than another heavier cross is put upon its shoulders . . . the Cross of humiliation." Was the country that had "uprooted totalitarianism . . . in just one wink of history" now to become "a victim on the altar of its own victory"? Romanians would not go begging at the "high imperial courts" of the West, he declared.

Perhaps not begging. But their government would definitely reach out, and to increasingly beneficial effect.

European Integration, U.S. Approval

Initially, the United States took an even harder line against the "new" Romania than did its European allies. In the aftermath of Ceauşescu's overthrow in December 1989, Washington appeared to find fault with the "neocommunist" character of the new regime. Secretary of State James Baker III was the last senior Western official to visit Bucharest in the wake of the revolution, and he stayed for only a few hours. The United States extended $80 million in humanitarian assistance, but over the next few years resisted rewarding Romania with long-term economic aid and the coveted most favored nation (MFN) trading status. In addition, U.S. leaders tended to distance themselves from senior Romanian officials at diplomatic gatherings.

By contrast, Western Europe took a more pragmatic, "business-as-usual" approach, feeling that the best way to change Romania's behavior was with hands-on engagement. Former French president François Mitterrand became the first Western head of state to visit Bucharest in April 1991, and a year later Romania and Germany signed a treaty of friendship and cooperation. The leading European powers were motivated in part by the perception that Romania, for all its internal imperfections, remained a bulwark between the growing chaos to the west—where Yugoslavia was descending into bloody civil war—and the east, where the Soviet Union had dissolved into a patchwork of quarrelsome mini-states.

These fears were skillfully played upon by Romanian diplomats, led by Adrian Nastase, who served as foreign minister from 1990 to 1992, and his successor Teodor Melescanu. Their first major coup came in February 1993 when, after many months of negotiations, Romania became the fourth former Communist country to sign an association agreement with the European Community (EC). Premier Nicolae Vacaroiu signed the accord in his first trip abroad as Romania's head of government.

The EC began as an organization for economic cooperation between Western European nations. But more recently it has evolved into a force for political integration as well, a process that reached a milestone in November 1993 when the Maastricht Treaty took effect and the EC became the European Union (EU). Romania's association agreement aimed to eliminate trade barriers between it and the EU over a 10-year period, though the process continues to lag far behind that schedule. But the accord also had an important symbolic value, as it began the process of ushering Romania into the political structures of modern Europe.

Another key step in that process came in October 1993, when Romania finally won admission to the Council of Europe as its 32nd full member. The Council of Europe, based in Strasbourg, France, is primarily a symbolic body, but membership in it is widely seen as a "passport" to other European political and economic institutions. Doubts about Romania's human rights record, particularly its treatment of its Hungarian (Magyar) minority, were the main reason that Romania was the last former Eastern bloc country to gain admission to the council. During months of hard negotiations Romania was compelled to promise to improve its record, and its membership won final approval in a meeting of the council's Committee of Ministers in which the Hungarian ambassador abstained in the voting.

In January 1994 Romania became the first former member of the Warsaw Pact—the Soviet-led defense alliance that dissolved in 1991—to sign an agreement with the North Atlantic Treaty Organization (NATO) under its new Partnership for Peace (PFP) program. NATO was the U.S.-led alliance that had faced off against the Soviet bloc during the long years of the cold war. NATO had designed the partnership as a means of reassuring the new Eastern European governments without granting them full membership in NATO, a move Moscow initially warned it would view as a threat to its security. Partnership members would not be entitled to automatic protection under NATO's defensive umbrella, but would be able to join NATO in joint military exercises, peacekeeping missions, training, and defense planning.

Romania's growing acceptance in Europe helped improve its relations with the United States as well. Earlier, Romania had garnered considerable goodwill from Washington during the Persian Gulf conflict of 1990–91. Romania had fortuitously taken over the rotating presidency of the United Nations Security Council a day before the Iraqi invasion of Kuwait and skillfully used its position to support the U.S.-led alliance against Iraq. The diplomatic respect it gained as a result was widely seen as having offset the large economic losses Romania suffered as a result of the UN's trade sanctions against Iraq.

The gradual thaw in U.S.-Romanian relations grew warmer still in October 1993, when the U.S. Congress voted in favor of ratifying a bilat-

Pope John Paul II embraces Romanian Orthodox Patriarch Teoctist in Bucharest during his historic visit to Romania in May 1999. He was the first pope to visit a mostly Orthodox Christian country in a millennium. (AP/Wide World Photos)

eral trade agreement that would include restoration of most favored nation trading status, long a key goal of Romanian foreign policy. That was followed in 1994 by a visit to Washington by President Iliescu, where he met with President Bill Clinton.

Three years later, in July 1997, President Clinton made a brief stopover in Bucharest during a European tour. "Stay the course and Romania will cross the milestone" of membership in NATO, Clinton told a cheering crowd of 100,000 that had been treated to free Coca-Cola and popcorn.

And in yet another diplomatic advance, Pope John Paul visited Romania on May 7–9, 1999, becoming the first pope to travel to a predominantly Orthodox Christian country since the Eastern and Western branches of Christianity split in the Great Schism of 1054. During his tour, the pontiff met with Patriarch Teoctist, leader of Romania's Orthodox Church, and President Emil Constantinescu.

A Good Neighbor Policy?

Romania understandably views itself as living in a rough neighborhood. Thus its efforts to improve its relations with Western Europe and the United States (aside from achieving economic benefits) are aimed at gaining protection against its historic enemies, such as Russia, Hungary, and Bulgaria.

Romania was the first former Soviet bloc nation to sign a treaty of friendship with Russia, which committed both countries to respect their mutual territorial integrity and the inviolability of their current borders. But bilateral tensions persisted over the issue of the former Soviet republic of Moldova, which gained its independence in 1991. Moldova controls most of the territory of the former Romanian province of Bessarabia (Ukraine controls the rest), which was part of Great Romania between the world wars. The majority of its population consists of ethnic Romanians, although there is a significant minority of ethnic Slavs, both Russians and Ukrainians.

There is a strong popular feeling among nationalist Romanians that Moldova should once again be reunited with its motherland. Anti-Russian slogans such as "Jackboots out of Moldova!" and "Russia is yours, Romania is ours" were commonly heard in Bucharest after the

1989 revolution. The Romanian government established diplomatic relations with Moldova in 1991 and steered clear of openly calling for reunification to avoid antagonizing Moscow. But in 1992 a civil war erupted when separatist Russians and Ukrainians in the eastern, primarily Slavic region of Trans-Dniester broke away from Moldova and declared independence. The Russian military lent support to the rebels, while Romania was reported to have supplied arms to the Moldovan forces.

The fighting ended in a stalemate, although Trans-Dniester retained de facto autonomy. In the years that followed, Moscow made moves to improve its relations with Moldova and withdraw support for the separatists. Meanwhile, Moldova held a national referendum in March 1994 in which some 95 percent of participating voters backed an independent state rather than union with Romania. That appeared to quash any remaining hopes in Bucharest for a merger between the two countries, at least for the foreseeable future.

Though relations between the two states gradually improved in what was called the "bridges of flowers" policy, things soured in 2001 and 2002. The Moldovan government accused Romania of using the Orthodox Church to interfere in its internal affairs, and responded by not recognizing the church and floating a plan to make its Romanian-speaking majority learn Russian in school. Both sides expelled in each other's diplomats as a result of the dispute.

Other territorial claims complicated Romania's relations with Ukraine and Bulgaria. Ukraine initially reacted angrily when Romanian nationalists raised the issue of former Romanian territories that Ukraine gained control of as a result of World War II, and Bulgaria accused Bucharest of having territorial designs on the region of southern Dobruja.

Despite these difficulties, Romania forged ahead with an energetic program of diplomacy in 1992; it opened an embassy in the Ukrainian capital of Kiev (and finally signed a treaty five years later), concluded a treaty with Bulgaria, and signed a series of agreements with Turkey and Greece. And in a significant early development, in June 1992, Romania and 10 of its neighbors (including six former Soviet republics) signed the so-called Declaration of Istanbul, which provided for the creation of a new zone of peaceful economic activity. This Black Sea Economic Cooperation Group was aimed at encouraging trade and developing transport and infrastructure in the region.

The major stumbling block to regional cooperation was the long-festering dispute between Romania and Hungary over Transylvania. Romania believed that Hungary still hoped to regain the territory and was using Transylvania's Magyar minority as a subversive "fifth column" to further that ultimate goal. Hungary in turn complained continually about what it saw as the Romanian government's political and cultural oppression of its ethnic brethren in Transylvania.

Nevertheless, both countries were determined to reach some sort of compromise in order to avoid hindering their efforts to gain greater integration into Europe. In September 1993 Geza Jeszenszky became the first Hungarian foreign minister to pay an official visit to Bucharest since 1989, and Romania's Foreign Minister Teodor Melescanu followed with a visit to Budapest in September 1994.

Finally, the two sides signed a treaty in September 1996 under which Hungary dropped its demand for autonomy for Romania's 1.6 million Magyar minority in exchange for Bucharest's commitment to guarantee them equal rights, despite bitter opposition from Romanian ultranationalists. Then in May 1997, Hungarian President Árpád Goncz paid an unprecedented visit to his country's historic enemy in which he pledged his government's support for Romania's bid to join NATO. In fact, the agreement figured to help both sides with their efforts to gain further entré into the European establishment.

Romania was motivated to improve its relations with its neighbors in part to compensate for the growing instability in the Balkans, the main reason for which was the civil wars that ripped apart Yugoslavia beginning in the early 1990s. Bucharest tried to present itself as a mediator in the conflicts between the rump Yugoslav federation (consisting of Serbia and Montenegro) and the newly independent republics of Croatia and Bosnia-Herzegovina.

The situation was complicated by Romania's efforts to enforce the U.N. embargo on Yugoslavia by preventing Serbia-bound vessels from proceeding up the Danube River. In late 1992 and early 1993, Serbian authorities retaliated by blockading the Danube, detaining Romanian tugboats and barges, and ordering the giant lock at the Iron Gates hydroelectric station to be closed to Romanian vessels. This so-called "ship-and-locks war" caused major economic losses to Romania and seemed to have a sobering effect on Bucharest. Although Romania reaffirmed its commitment to upholding the U.N. sanctions, it proceeded in April 1994 to sign a treaty with Yugoslavia—which had become an international pariah state—on bilateral political relations.

However, as the United States and NATO became more deeply involved the conflicts in the former Yugoslavia in the years that followed, first in Bosnia and then in the Serbian province of Kosovo, Romania was forced to choose sides more directly. After hedging for a number of months, the government in the spring of 1999 finally granted NATO the right to use Romania's airspace without restrictions in its intervention against Yugoslav forces in Kosovo and Serbia.

Many average Romanians were not happy with the U.S.-led attack against a traditional ally and trading partner, and especially with the heavy bombing of civilian industrial targets in Belgrade that caused serious pollution of the Danube River and other economic disruptions. But by throwing their lot in openly with the West, and by later contributing Romanian troops to the UN forces in Bosnia and Kosovo, Bucharest was laying the groundwork for further cooperation that would rise to new levels following a most unexpected event—one which occurred far from southeastern Europe.

The World After 9/11

That day in 2001 now known as 9/11—the September 11 hijackings and suicide attacks on the World Trade Center and the Pentagon—had reverberations far beyond America's shores. For Romania, it was a chance to demonstrate to Washington once and for all that it could be a reliable ally, both in the unstable Balkans and in the so-called war on terror.

In the immediate aftermath of 9/11, Bucharest announced its readiness to assist in any way possible. By early 2002, a small force of Romanian policemen and military officers had already been dispatched to Afghanistan to aid the U.S.-dominated force that had intervened there against the al-Qaeda terrorists blamed for 9/11 and their Taliban allies. That summer, a larger 400-man force of infantry soldiers, the Red Scorpions, deployed to the Kandahar airbase to man joint patrols with U.S. forces.

"You can count the number of Romanian officers who have studied in the United States in the hundreds, if not in the thousands," said a U.S.

Army adviser with Romania's defense ministry. Noting how much things had changed in the past decade, the officer added that when his flight from Bucharest to Afghanistan stopped in the former Soviet republic of Turkmenistan to refuel, "we had a hard time finding anyone on board who spoke Russian."

As a further gesture, in August 2002 Romania became the first country to pledge not to surrender American citizens to the new International Criminal Court. The court had been recently established under an international treaty that President Bush had withdrawn the U.S. from, saying he feared it would subject Americans to political prosecution.

"We play the American card, and aggressively," admitted Silviu Brucan, the former communist who was now one of Romania's elder statesmen. As for charges that Bucharest was exploiting the tragedy of 9/11 for diplomatic gain, Defense Minister Ioan Mircea Pascu replied: "There was no gambling on corpses, as we are accused."

Romania's demonstrations of solidarity with Washington paid off that November, when it was one of seven former Soviet-bloc nations that were formally invited to join NATO in 2004. Two days later, on November 23, Bush stopped in Bucharest and spoke briefly before a large crowd in Revolution Square. He suggested that because Romanians had seen "the face of evil" under Nicolae Ceauşescu, they understood the dangers allegedly posed by Iraqi president Saddam Hussein's regime, which Bush had vowed to disarm and remove by force.

"The people of Romania understand that aggressive dictators cannot be appeased or ignored; they must always be opposed," Bush declared.

However, the new-found "special relationship" with Washington carried the risk of alienating Romania from key members of the European Union, which were unhappy with many Bush administration policies, including its stance on Iraq. Some European officials expressed concern that Romania's success on security issues might allow it to think it could escape enacting the deeper economic and political reforms needed before it could join the EU.

Some Romanians agreed. "The average Romanian has very little to gain from joining NATO [as opposed to the EU], which is something rarely heard," said investment banker Matei Paun.

In any event, it doesn't appear Romania will be joining the EU any time soon. In October 2002, European leaders announced that 10 countries were on track to become members in 2004. But they took a much more go-slow and cautious approach to Romania and Bulgaria, merely saying they "noted" the two countries' desire to join by 2007 and expressing a commitment to help them reach that goal.

NOTES

pp. 145–146 " 'In December 1989, Romania . . .' " Nestor Ratesh, *Romania: The Entangled Revolution*, pp. 148–149.

p. 146 " 'A new martyrdom begins for Romania. . . .' " Mark Frankland, *The Patriots' Revolution*, p. 194

p. 149 " 'Stay the course and Romania . . .' " Nicola Williams, *Romania & Moldova*, p. 31.

p. 151 " 'ships-and-locks war' " Williams, p. 31.

p. 152 " 'You can count the number of Romanian . . .' " James Brooke, *New York Times*, September 22, 2002.

p. 153 " 'There was no gambling on corpses . . .' " Ian Fisher, *New York Times*, October 23, 2002.

p. 153 " 'The people of Romania understand that . . .' " The White House. "President Bush Welcomes Romania to NATO." Available on-line. URL: http://www.whitehouse.gov/news/releases/2002/11/print/2002/23-7.html. Downloaded on December 29, 2002.

p. 153 " 'The average Romanian has very little to gain . . .' " Fisher, *New York Times*.

12

FUTURE PROSPECTS

The paradox of Romania has been that it is a nation obsessed with its history and identity while being unable to come to terms with either. But if the country is to build on the halting progress it has made in the nearly 15 years since the revolution, Romanian people must look honestly in their collective mirror, and insist that their government do the same.

It will not be easy, for their tortured past has taught Romanians to often look to outside forces to either save them or to blame for their misfortunes. Certainly they will require the goodwill and assistance of the international community to succeed, but in the end they will need most of all to rely on their own inner strengths as a people, strengths that have in fact developed as a direct result of their harrowing history.

"Some countries are blessed with a sort of grace: everything works for them, even their misfortunes and catastrophes," according to the late Romanian writer E. M. Cioran. "There are others for whom nothing succeeds and whose very triumphs are but failures. When they try to assert themselves and take a step forward, some external fate intervenes to break their momentum and return them to their starting point."

Others have similarly noted that the story of Romania is a concrete illustration of the Greek myth of Sisyphus, the ancient king who was punished by having to continually push a huge boulder up a hill, only to have it roll back down to the bottom each time he reached the summit. Romania's history is replete with such reverses, especially in the 20th century. The dream of Greater Romania is born after World War I but disappears after World War II amid a Soviet-imposed Communist takeover. Hopes are briefly reawakened by a breakaway from the Soviet orbit but quickly dashed by the descent into the darkness of the Ceauşescu dictatorship. Finally, with the 1989 revolution Romanian society is once again put in the position of starting over from scratch.

However, the picture is certainly far from one of unreserved gloom. Since the early 1990s, there has now been a succession of mostly fair national elections that have resulted in changes of government with a minimum of violence or other popular unrest. There is very little political repression by the state, the press is lively and free, and people can express their opinions openly without fear of repercussions. These are tangible and impressive achievements that all Romanians can be proud of.

But the people themselves will be the first to say that the revolution has to a large extent failed to provide a decent way of life for them and their children. Despite the efforts of both left-wing (some would say neo-communist) and conservative governments, the standard of living for many people—particularly in such basic areas as income, health care, and housing—is little better if not actually worse than it was under communism. The fact that among some Romanians there is a degree of nostalgia for the Ceauşescu era is a sad and telling development.

Modest progress, to put it charitably, has been made on the economic-reform front, but Romania still remains further from a genuine market economy than almost any other formerly communist country in Eastern Europe. The common people have suffered under a host of International Monetary Fund-mandated adjustment programs. Direct foreign investment that could create new jobs remains miniscule compared to foreign investment in Romania's neighbors, in large part because of Romania's perceived corruption.

As a result, Bucharest has put much of its hope into its eventual admission into the European Union. "Eventual" is certainly the word, for while membership would benefit the country immensely, the EU is clearly reluctant to take on the expense and political headaches that would be involved in trying to integrate far-off Romania into modern Europe. In the shorter term, the government looks to leverage its new post-September 11 relationship with Washington into accelerated membership in the North Atlantic Treaty Organization. Some have expressed concerns that Romania will use its perceived value as a military ally to avoid having to make harder decisions on economic reform.

Ultimately, however, whatever happens on the international scene, it will be up to regular Romanians to steer the destiny of their country onto a new course. They can no longer simply put the burden on others, whether they be in foreign capitals or in their own government. Centuries of misrule have caused many Romanians both to blame perceived outsiders in Romanian society—Turk, Jew, Gypsy, Hungarian—for their problems. At the same time they rely on a self-interested elite to run their affairs. Some people (both progressive-minded Romanians and sympathetic foreign voices) are now saying it is past time for a change.

Some have called for their countrymen to begin coming to terms with the twin impulses of national chauvinism and scapegoating that contributed both to the holocaust of Romania's Jews in World War II and to the strong support for a neofascist presidential candidate in the 2000 elections. Some have also urged Romanians to apply to see the files that the Securitate compiled on them during the years of communism in order to see how virtually the whole country cooperated in its own repression under Ceauşescu.

The National Council for Research on the Archives of the Securitate was set up in 1999, but only in the last two years has it been possible for regular Romanians to apply to see their files. Bureaucratic hurdles remain, however, and as of October 2002, only 862 people our of 7,208 applicants had actually gotten a look at their dossier. "All Romanians should get to know their files as a way of healing themselves of this evil," one author said.

Nevertheless, interest appears slight, perhaps because the files amount to an indictment of much of Romanian society during Ceauşescu's reign. According to one study, of the estimated 600,000 informers recruited by the Securitate over the decades to spy on their neighbors, 39 percent were university-educated, 37 percent were high school graduates, and a whopping 97 percent were neither paid nor blackmailed but were simply motivated by "political and patriotic feeling."

Dealing with such collective guilt and amnesia is not easy, says former dissident Doina Cornea, "because everything has a price and few people are ready to pay this price." But if Romanians want to demand more of their government, they may first have to demand more of themselves and their fellow citizens.

The glorious month of December 1989 "was a revolution in people's souls when they suddenly felt no more fear," Andrei Codrescu has written. "This revolution is going on still." If Romanians can gradually come to terms with their own history, perhaps that revolution can finally be carried through and completed, so their country can at last join modern Europe as an equal, without fear or favor.

NOTES

p. 155 "'Some countries are blessed with a sort of grace: . . .'" Tony Judt, *New York Review of Books*, November 1, 2001.

p. 157 "'All Romanians should get to know their files . . .'" Mirel Bran, *Le Monde*, October 8, 2002. Available on-line. URL: http://www.worldpress.org/article_model.cfm?article_id=877&dont=yes. Downloaded on December 29, 2002.

p. 157 "'because everything has a price and few people . . .'" Bran.

p. 158 "'was a revolution in people's souls . . .'" Andrei Codrescu, *The Hole in the Flag*, p. 238.

CHRONOLOGY

The Pre-Modern Era

A.D. 101–106
Kingdom of Dacia conquered by Roman emperor Trajan

A.D. 271
Emperor Aurelian orders Roman withdrawal

3rd–6th centuries
Succession of invasions by barbarian tribes from the East

896
Magyars arrive in Hungary and subsequently absorb Transylvania

1360
Moldavia declares independence from Hungary

1380
Walachia follows suit

1386–1418
Rule of Mircea the Old in Walachia

1437
Transylvania's noblemen form Union of Three Nations

1456–62

Rule of Vlad Tepes (the Impaler) in Walachia

1457–1504

Rule of Stephen the Great in Moldavia

1521–41

Ottoman Turks consolidate control of Romanian lands

1593–1601

Rule of Michael the Brave, who briefly unites Romania

1699

Uniate Church founded in Transylvania

1711–16

Turks institute Phanariot system in Moldavia and Walachia

1711–1856

Russia, Austria, and Ottoman Empire wage wars on Romanian soil

1821

Revolt ends Phanariot system

The Modern Era

1859–66

Rule of Alexander Cuza

1861

Union of Moldavia and Walachia

1866–1914

Rule of King Carol I

1881

Kingdom of Romania declared

1907

Peasant revolt crushed

1912–13

First and Second Balkan Wars fought

1914–27

Rule of King Ferdinand I

1918

World War I ends. Greater Romania formed

1921

Romanian Communist Party (RCP) founded

1930–40

Rule of King Carol II

1940

June–August: Greater Romania dismembered at start of World War II
September: Fascist Marshal Ion Antonescu seizes power

1944

August: King Michael ousts Antonescu in anti-German coup; Soviet army moves in

The Communist Era

1945

March 6: Pro-Communist Petru Groza named premier
October 1945: Gheorghe Gheorghiu-Dej becomes Romanian Communist Party general secretary

1946

November: RCP wins power in fraudulent elections

1947

February 10: Treaty of Paris recognizes Romania's postwar borders
December 30: King Michael forced to abdicate; People's Republic of Romania proclaimed

1948

March: RCP consolidates power in national elections

1948–62

Agricultural system forcibly collectivized

1952

Gheorghiu-Dej consolidates position as undisputed leader

1956

Romania begins to chart international course independent of Soviet Union

1964

April 26: Central Committee issues "Declaration of Independence" from Moscow

1965

March 19: Gheorghiu-Dej dies; succeeded by triumvirate from which Nicolae Ceauşescu ultimately emerges on top

1967

Romania establishes relations with West Germany; retains ties with Israel after Six Day War

1968

Ceauşescu wins Western praise by opposing Soviet invasion of Czechoslovakia

1971

Ceauşescus visit China and North Korea; are inspired to create cult of personality and "pharaonic socialism"

1988

Rural "systemization" program prompts crisis with Hungary; Ceauşescu renounces most-favored-nation (MFN) trading status with U.S.

1989

March: "Letter of Six" criticizing Ceauşescu issued by former leading officials

December 15–20: Timişoara racked by protests and bloodshed

December 22–25: Unrest spreads to Bucharest; Ceauşescus flee and are captured; National Salvation Front (NSF) proclaimed

December 25: Nicolae and Elena Ceauşescu executed

The Post-Communist Era

1990

January: Anticommunist protests against NSF erupt

May 20: NSF triumphs in mostly free elections; Ion Iliescu becomes president

June 14–15: Government imports Jiu Valley coal miners to crush opposition and "restore order"

August: National Agency for Privatization set up

November: Price increases prompt 100,000-strong protest in Bucharest

1991

September: Jiu Valley miners return to confront government; Premier Petre Roman forced to resign and is replaced by Theodor Stolojan

November: Parliament approves new constitution defining Romania as a multiparty presidential republic with a free-market economy

December: New constitution endorsed by 77 percent of voters in national referendum

1992

February–March: Local elections confirm decline in popularity of NSF

March: NSF formally splits into two parties; leftist faction retains power while centrist faction goes into opposition

April: Exiled King Michael receives tumultuous welcome during brief visit to Bucharest

June: Romania joins 11-nation Black Sea Economic Cooperation Group

September: Ruling Democratic National Salvation Front (DNSF) hangs onto power in national elections

October: Iliescu wins presidential runoff vote

November: Nicolae Vacaroiu named premier

1993

February: Romania signs association agreement with the European Community

July: DNSF merges with smaller leftist parties to form ruling Party of Social Democracy in Romania (PSDR)

October: Romania wins admission to the Council of Europe

November: Huge pro-economic reform protest staged in Bucharest

1994

January: Romania joins NATO's Partnership for Peace program

April: The national currency, the leu, is "floated" (becomes internally convertible with other currencies)

August: Extremist right-wing Party of Romanian National Unity (PRNU) officially joins government

October: King Michael denied entry at Bucharest airport

1995

January: Ruling PSDR formally cements alliance with three extremist ultranationalist parties

1996

September: Romania and Hungary sign treaty settling border disputes and protecting ethnic minorities

October: Ruling PSDR ousts ultranationalists from cabinet after their leader calls the Hungary treaty "treason"

November: Center-right DCR coalition defeats PSDR in national elections. Emil Constantinescu defeats Ion Iliescu in runoff to become president

1997

May: Hungarian President Árpád Goncz pays state visit to Romania

July: U.S. president Bill Clinton makes stopover in Bucharest

1998

March: Premier Victor Ciorba resigns and is replaced by Radu Vasile

1999

January: Jiu Valley miners again march on Bucharest and clash violently with police; reach deal with government

April: Romania grants NATO right to use airspace in attacks on Kosovo and Serbia

May: Pope John Paul II travels to Romania; first pope to visit an Orthodox country since 1054

December: Vasile resigns as premier and is replaced by Mugur Isarescu

2000

January–February: Tons of cyanide-laden sludge from a Romanian gold mine flows into the Szamos, Tisza, and Danube Rivers in one of Europe's worst-ever aquatic accidents

May: National Investment Fund collapses amid embezzlement charges; thousands lose life savings

November: Opposition PSD (formerly PSDR) defeats DCR-led government in national elections. Ultranationalist Corneliu Vadim Tudor finishes close behind Ion Iliescu

December: Iliescu defeats Tudor in runoff and returns to presidency. Adrian Nastase named premier

2001

October: Government imposes one-year ban on foreign adoptions of Romanian children; ban later extended to 2003

September–December: Romania takes numerous steps to line up behind the United States after September 11 terrorist attacks

2002

January–December: Romanian forces deploy to Afghanistan as part of "war on terror"

August: Government pledges not to surrender any United States citizens to new International Criminal Court

November: Romania invited to join NATO in 2004; President Bush visits Bucharest

FURTHER READING

BOOKS

Bachman, Ronald D., ed. *Romania: A Country Study*. Washington, D.C.: Library of Congress, 1991.

Banac, Ivo, ed. *Eastern Europe in Revolution*. Ithaca, N.Y.: Cornell University Press, 1992.

Basdevant, Denise. *Against Tide and Tempest: The Story of Romania*. New York: Robert Spellers & Sons, 1965.

Behr, Edward. *Kiss the Hand You Cannot Bite: The Rise and Fall of the Ceauşescus*. New York: Villard Books, 1991.

Bobango, Gerald J. *The Emergence of the Romanian National State*. Boulder, Colo.: East European Quarterly, 1979.

Boia, Lucian. *Romania: Borderland of Europe (Topographics)*. London: Reaktion Books, 2002.

Brown, Aurel. *Romanian Foreign Policy Since 1965*. New York: Praeger, 1978.

Brown, J. F. *Eastern Europe and Communist Rule*. Durham, N.C.: Duke University Press, 1988.

———. *The New Eastern Europe: The Khrushchev Era and After*. New York: Praeger, 1966

Cartwright, Andrew. *The Return of the Peasant: Land Reform in Post-Communist Romania*. Aldershot, U.K.: Ashgate Publishing, 2001.

Cipkowski, Peter. *Revolution in Eastern Europe*. New York: John Wiley & Sons, 1991.

Codrescu, Andrei. *The Hole in the Flag: A Romanian Exile's Story of Return and Revolution*. New York: William Morrow, 1991.

Fischer-Galati, Stephen. *The New Rumania: From People's Democracy to Socialist Republic*. Cambridge, Mass.: MIT Press, 1967.

Florescu, Radu, and McNally, Raymond. *Dracula, Price of Many Faces: His Life and His Times*. New York: Little Brown, 1999.

Frankland, Mark. *The Patriots' Revolution: How Eastern Europe Toppled Communism and Won Its Freedom*. Chicago: Ivan Dee, 1992.

Giurescu, Constantin C. *Transylvania in the History of Romania: An Historical Outline*. London: Garnstone Press.

Gursan-Salzman. *The Last Jews of Radauti*. Garden City, N.Y.: Doubleday, 1983.

Hale, Julian. *The Land and People of Romania*. Philadelphia: J. B. Lippincott, 1972.

Hoffman, Charles. *Gray Dawn: The Jews of Eastern Europe in the Post-Communist Era*. New York: HarperCollins, 1992.

Hoffman, Eva. *Exit into History: A Journey Through the New Eastern Europe*. New York: Viking, 1993.

Ioanid, Radu. *The Holocaust in Romania: The Destruction of Jews and Gypsies Under the Antonescu Regime, 1940–1944*. Chicago: Ivan R. Dee, 2000.

Jagendorf, Siegfried. *Jagendorf's Foundry: A Memoir of the Romanian Holocaust, 1941–1944*. New York: HarperCollins, 1991.

Kligman, Gail. *The Politics of Duplicity: Controlling Reproduction in Ceauşescu's Romania*. Berkeley: University of California Press, 1998.

Laufer, Peter. *Iron Curtain Rising*. San Francisco: Mercury House, 1991.

Lendvai, Paul. *Eagles in Cobwebs: Nationalism and Communism in the Balkans*. Garden City, N.Y.: Doubleday, 1969.

Levy, Robert. *Ana Pauker: the Rise and Fall of a Jewish Communist*. Berkeley: University of California Press, 2001.

Light, Duncan and Phinnemore, David, eds. *Post-Communist Romania: Coming to Terms With Transition*. Basingstoke, U.K.: Palgrave Macmillan, 2001.

Manea, Norman. *On Clowns: The Dictator and the Artist*. New York: Grove Weidenfeld, 1992.

Otetea, Andrei, ed. *The History of the Romanian People*. New York: Twayne Publishers, 1970.

Popescu, Petru. *The Return*. San Antonio: Grove Press, 1997.

Ratesh, Nestor. *Romania: The Entangled Revolution*. New York: Praeger & the Center for Strategic and International Studies, 1991.

Shafir, Michael. *Romania—Politics, Economics and Society: Political Stagnation and Simulated Change*. Boulder, Colo.: Lynne Rienner Publishers, 1985.

Stokes, Gale. *The Walls Came Tumbling Down: The Collapse of Communism in Eastern Europe*. New York: Oxford University Press, 1993.

Tismaneanu, Vladimir. *Reinventing Politics: Eastern Europe from Stalin to Havel*. New York: Macmillan, 1992.

Verdery, Katherine. *National Ideology Under Socialism: Identity and Cultural Politics in Ceauşescu's Romania*. Berkeley: University of California Press, 1995.

Williams, Nicola, et al. *Romania & Moldova*. Victoria, Australia: Lonely Planet, 2001.

PERIODICALS

(Note: In the listings below, *Radio Free Europe/Radio Liberty Research Reports* has been abbreviated as *RFE/RL*. Beginning in 1995 that journal became *Transition*.)

Barany, Zoltan. "Grim Realities in Eastern Europe." *Transition*, March 29, 1995, 3–8.

Barth, Jack. "In Search of Dracula." *Travel & Leisure*, December 1994, 82.

Binder, David. "European Gypsies Issue Call For Human Rights." *New York Times*, May 2, 1993, A12.

Brooke, James. "Romanians Join American Patrols in Afghanistan." *New York Times*, September 22, 2002, A13.

Bumiller, Elisabeth. "Bush Appeals to New Allies on Iraq Plans." *New York Times*, November 24, 2002, A1.

Codrescu, Andrei. "Fascism on a Pedestal." *New York Times*, December 7, 1993, A27.

Economist, Editors of. "Isarescued." *Economist*, July 9, 1994, 53.

Erlanger, Steven. "Ex-President of Romania Is Favored In Vote Today." *New York Times*, February 11, 2001, A6.

Fisher, Ian. "Romania Pins Hope for NATO Seat on U.S. Friendship." *New York Times*, October 23, 2002, A9.

Henry, David C. "Reviving Romania's Rural Economy." *RFE/RL*, February 18, 1994, 18–24.

Ingram, Judith. "Now Romania Aids Orphans At Its Hearth." *New York Times*, July 25, 1994, A9.

Ionescu, Dan. "Birth Pangs of Privatization." *Transition*, April 14, 1995. 47–51.

———. "UM 0215: A Controversial Intelligence Service in Romania." *RFE/RL*, July 29, 1994, 27–30.

———. "Personnel Changes in the Romanian Intelligence Service." *RFE/RL*, July 8, 1994, 22–25.

———. "Romania Adjusting to NATO's Partnership for Peace Program." *RFE/RL*, March 4, 1994, 43–47.

———. "Romania's Privatization Program: Who Is in Charge?" *RFE/RL*, February 4, 1994, 28–34.

———. "Romania's Currency Plummeting." *RFE/RL*, December 10, 1993, 43–48.

———. "Romania Admitted to the Council of Europe." *RFE/RL*, November 5, 1993, 40–45.

———. "Still No Breakthrough in Romanian-Hungarian Relations." *RFE/RL*, October 22, 1993, 26–32.

———. "Health Care Crisis: Romania." *RFE/RL*, October 8, 1993, 60–62.

———. "The Balkan Conflict: Romania's Quandary." *RFE/RL*, March 9, 1993, 13–17.

———. "Romania Signs Association Agreement with the EC." *RFE/RL*, March 5, 1993, 33–37.

———. "Romania's Winter of Shortages." *RFE/RL*, February 5, 1993, 45–48.

Judt, Tony. "Romania: Bottom of the Heap." *The New York Review of Books*, November 1, 2001.

Kamm, Henry. "End of Communism Worsens Anti-Gypsy Racism." *New York Times*, November 17, 1993, A12.

———. "Death Is a Neighbor, and the Gypsies Are Terrified." *New York Times*, October 27, 1993, A4.

McNeil Jr., Donald G. "Romania Seeks to Stay On the Track to Europe." *New York Times*, December 10, 2000, A8.

Nash, Nathaniel C. "From Communist Vineyards, A Bouquet of Iodine." *New York Times*, March 8, 1995, A4.

———. "Coke's Great Romanian Adventure." *New York Times*, February 26, 1995, F1.

Ottaway, David B. "Post-Communist Country a Pre-Industrial Time Warp." *Washington Post*, August 1, 1994, A17.

———. "A Battle for Identity Divides Transylvania." *Washington Post*, July 5, 1994, A12.

Perlez, Jane. "Uprising or Coup? Romanians Ask 5 Years Later." *New York Times*, December 25, 1994, A3.

———. "Where Communists Trampled, a Village Rises." *New York Times*, October 18, 1994, A4.

———. "Romanian Leader Calls Ex-King a Threat." *New York Times*, October 13, 1994, A5.

———. "A Suitably Opaque Talk With Romania's Top Spy." *New York Times*, November 30, 1993, A4.

———. "Bleak Romanian Economy Growing Ever Bleaker." *New York Times*, November 24, 1993, A3.

Shafir, Michael. "Ruling Party Formalizes Relations With Extremists." *Transition*, April 14, 1995, 42–46.

———. "Immigrants in Romania." *RFE/RL*, June 24, 1994, 41–46.

———. "Romania." *RFE/RL*, April 22, 1994, 87–94.

———. "Best-selling Spy Novels Seek to Rehabilitate Romanians' Securitate." *RFE/RL*, November 12, 1993, 14–18.

———. "The Caritas Affair: A Transylvanian 'Eldorado,'" *RFE/RL*, September 24, 1993, 23–27.

———. "Romanians and the Transition to Democracy." *RFE/RL*, April 30, 1993, 42–48.

————. "Growing Political Extremism in Romania." *RFE/RL*, April 2, 1993, 18–25.

Shafir, Michael, and Dan Ionescu. "Romania: A Crucially Uneventful Year." *RFE/RL*, January 7, 1994, 122–126.

————. "Romania: Political Change and Economic Malaise." *RFE/RL*, January 1, 1993, 108–112.

Thurow, Roger. "Miners Can Move Mountains in Romania." *Wall Street Journal*, October 20, 1994, A19.

Washington Post, Editors of. "Transcript of the Closed Trial of Nicolae and Elena Ceaușescu." *Washington Post*, December 29, 1989, A26.

ON-LINE SOURCES

Bran, Mirel. "In the Mirror of Romania's Defunct Secret Police, Former Dissident Sees an Image of Herself" *Le Monde* October 8, 2002. Available on-line. URL: http://www.worldpress.org/article_model.cfm?article_id=877&dont=yes.

Habitat World. "Habitat House Yields Stability." The Publication of Habitat for Humanity International, April–May 2002. Available on-line. URL: http://www.habitat.org/hw/april-may02/feature_7.html.

Holt, Ed. "Ceaușescu Beats Dracula to Bring New Blood into Romanian Tourism," *Scotland on Sunday*. Available on-line. URL: http://www.scotlandonsunday.com/international.cfm?id=1422262002. Posted on December 22, 2002.

Kirka, Danica. "Romanian Children Wanted—but not Available." *Miami Herald*. Available on-line. URL: http://www.miami.com/mld/miamiherald/news/world/4831391.htm. Posted on Dec. 29, 2002.

Lovatt, Catherine. "Nations in Transit 2001: Romania." Freedom House. August 12, 2002. Available on-line. URL: http://www.freedomhouse.org/research/nattransit.htm. Downloaded on October 12, 2002.

McKinsey, Kitty. "Bulgaria/Romania: A Study of Two Failing Health-Care Systems." *RFE/RL*. May 20, 1997. Available on-line. URL: http://www.rferl.org/nca/features/1997/05/F.RU.97052090817.html. Downloaded on February 3, 2003.

Simpson, Daniel, "Elie Wiesel Asks a Haunted Hometown to Face Up," *New York Times*. Available on-line URL: http://www.nytimes.com/2002/07/.../31ROMA.html. Posted August 2, 2002.

Shafir, Michael. "Romania: Government Comes to Mysterious Agreement With Miners," *RFE/RL*. Available on-line. URL: http://www.rferl.org/nca/features/1999/01/F.RU.990127134446.html. Posted on January 27, 1999.

Tomiuc, Eugen. "Romania: Dracula Park Expected to Pump Fresh Blood Into Ailing Tourism Industry," *RFE/RL*. November 11, 2001. Available on-line.

URL: http://www.rferl.org/nca/features/2001/11/0811200182145.asp. Posted on Nov. 11, 2001.

United Nations Economic Commission for Europe. "Housing Market Alone Cannot Accommodate All Romanians." Country profile issued on April 9, 2002. Available on-line. URL: http://www.un.ro/English-hm.doc.

U.S. Department of State. "Romania: Country Reports on Human Rights Practices—2000." February 23, 2001. U.S. Department of State. Available on-line. URL. http://www.state.gov/g/drl/rls/hrrpt/2000/eur/881.htm.

Zeller, Tom. "Hold the Bloody Mary," *New York Times*. Available on-line. URL: http://www.nytimes.com/2002/0…/26ZELL.html. Posted on May 26, 2002.

INDEX

Page numbers followed by *m* indicate maps, those followed by *i* indicate illustrations, and those followed by *c* indicate an item in the chronology.